TRADE ISSUES, POLICIES AND LAWS

ILLICIT TRADE IN WILDLIFE AND THE ECONOMICS OF AGRICULTURAL AND WILDLIFE SMUGGLING

TRADE ISSUES, POLICIES AND LAWS

Additional books in this series can be found on Nova's website
under the Series tab.

Additional E-books in this series can be found on Nova's website
under the E-book tab.

WILDLIFE PROTECTION, DESTRUCTION AND EXTINCTION

Additional books in this series can be found on Nova's website
under the Series tab.

Additional E-books in this series can be found on Nova's website
under the E-book tab.

TRADE ISSUES, POLICIES AND LAWS

ILLICIT TRADE IN WILDLIFE AND THE ECONOMICS OF AGRICULTURAL AND WILDLIFE SMUGGLING

ROLANDE GAGNIER
EDITOR

NOVINKA

New York

For permission to use material from this book please contact us:
Telephone 631-231-7269; Fax 631-231-8175
Web Site: http://www.novapublishers.com

Additional color graphics may be available in the e-book version of this book.

LIBRARY OF CONGRESS CATALOGING-IN-PUBLICATION DATA

ISBN: 978-1-62417-877-1

Published by Nova Science Publishers, Inc. † New York

CONTENTS

PREFACE

Global trade in illegal wildlife is a growing illicit economy, estimated to be worth at least $5 billion and potentially in excess of $20 billion annually. Some of the most lucrative illicit wildlife commodities include tiger parts, caviar, elephant ivory, rhino horn, and exotic birds and reptiles. Demand for illegally obtained wildlife is ubiquitous, and some suspect that illicit demand may be growing. This book provides an overview of illegal wildlife crime with a focus on determining funding levels for U.S. wildlife trade inspection and investigation; evaluating the effectiveness of U.S. foreign aid to combat the wildlife trade; using trade sanctions to penalize foreign countries with weak enforcement of wildlife laws; incorporating wildlife trade provisions into free trade agreements; and addressing the domestic and international demand for illegal wildlife through public awareness campaigns and non-governmental organization partnerships.

Chapter 1 – Global trade in illegal wildlife is a growing illicit economy, estimated to be worth at least $5 billion and potentially in excess of $20 billion annually. Some of the most lucrative illicit wildlife commodities include tiger parts, caviar, elephant ivory, rhino horn, and exotic birds and reptiles. Demand for illegally obtained wildlife is ubiquitous, and some suspect that illicit demand may be growing.

International wildlife smuggling may be of interest to Congress as it presents several potential environmental and national security threats to the United States. Threats to the environment include the potential loss of biodiversity, introduction of invasive species into U.S. ecosystems, and transmission of disease through illegal wildlife trade, including through illegal bushmeat trade. National security threats include links between wildlife trafficking and organized crime and drug trafficking. Some terrorist groups may also be seeking to finance their activities through illegal wildlife trade, according to experts. Wildlife source and transit countries may be especially prone to exploitation if known to have weak state capacity, poor law enforcement, corrupt governments, and porous borders.

The U.S. government addresses illegal wildlife trade through several national and international venues. Congress has passed numerous laws that regulate and restrict certain types of wildlife imports and exports, including the Endangered Species Act of 1973, the Lacey Act and Lacey Act Amendments of 1981, and several species-specific conservation laws. These laws and others establish authorities and guidelines for wildlife trade inspection at ports of entry, and wildlife crime law enforcement and prosecution. Internationally, the United States is party to several wildlife conservation treaties, including the United Nations Convention on International Trade in Endangered Species of Wild Fauna and Flora (CITES), which serves as the primary vehicle for regulating wildlife trade. Foreign training and assistance programs to combat illegal wildlife trade are also conducted by some federal agencies, including the U.S. Department of State, which leads an international initiative against wildlife trafficking.

The role of Congress in evaluating U.S. policy to combat wildlife trafficking is broad. Potential issues for Congress include (1) determining funding levels for U.S. wildlife trade inspection and investigation; (2) evaluating the effectiveness of U.S. foreign aid to combat wildlife trafficking; (3) developing ways to encourage private-sector involvement in regulating the wildlife trade; (4) using trade sanctions to penalize foreign countries with weak enforcement of wildlife laws; (5) incorporating wildlife trade provisions into free trade agreements; and (6) addressing the domestic and international demand for illegal wildlife through public awareness campaigns and non-governmental organization partnerships. This report focuses on the international trade in terrestrial fauna, largely excluding trade in illegal plants, including timber, and fish.

Chapter 2 – The United States bans imports of certain agricultural and wildlife goods that can carry pathogens or diseases or whose harvest can threaten wildlife stocks or endanger species. Despite these bans, contraband is regularly uncovered in inspections of cargo containers and in domestic markets.

This study characterizes the economic factors affecting agricultural and wildlife smuggling by drawing on inspection and interdiction data from USDA and the U.S. Fish and Wildlife Service and existing economic literature.

Findings reveal that agricultural and wildlife smuggling primarily include luxury goods, ethnic foods, and specialty goods, such as traditional medicines.

Incidents of detected smuggling are disproportionately higher for agricultural goods originating in China and for wildlife goods originating in Mexico.

Fragmentary data show that approximately 1 percent of all commercial wildlife shipments to the United States and 0.40 percent of all U.S. wildlife imports by value are refused entry and suspected of being smuggled.

In: Illicit Trade in Wildlife and the Economics ... ISBN: 978-1-62417-877-1
Editor: Rolande Gagnier

Chapter 1

INTERNATIONAL ILLEGAL TRADE IN WILDLIFE: THREATS AND U.S. POLICY*

Liana Sun Wyler and Pervaze A. Sheikh

SUMMARY

Global trade in illegal wildlife is a growing illicit economy, estimated to be worth at least $5 billion and potentially in excess of $20 billion annually. Some of the most lucrative illicit wildlife commodities include tiger parts, caviar, elephant ivory, rhino horn, and exotic birds and reptiles. Demand for illegally obtained wildlife is ubiquitous, and some suspect that illicit demand may be growing.

International wildlife smuggling may be of interest to Congress as it presents several potential environmental and national security threats to the United States. Threats to the environment include the potential loss of biodiversity, introduction of invasive species into U.S. ecosystems, and transmission of disease through illegal wildlife trade, including through illegal bushmeat trade. National security threats include links between wildlife trafficking and organized crime and drug trafficking. Some terrorist groups may also be seeking to finance their activities through illegal wildlife trade, according to experts. Wildlife source and transit countries may be especially prone to exploitation if known to have weak

---

* This is an edited, reformatted and augmented version of a Congressional Research Service publication, CRS Report for Congress RL34395, from www.crs.gov, prepared for Members and Committees of Congress, dated February 5, 2010.

state capacity, poor law enforcement, corrupt governments, and porous borders.

The U.S. government addresses illegal wildlife trade through several national and international venues. Congress has passed numerous laws that regulate and restrict certain types of wildlife imports and exports, including the Endangered Species Act of 1973, the Lacey Act and Lacey Act Amendments of 1981, and several species-specific conservation laws. These laws and others establish authorities and guidelines for wildlife trade inspection at ports of entry, and wildlife crime law enforcement and prosecution. Internationally, the United States is party to several wildlife conservation treaties, including the United Nations Convention on International Trade in Endangered Species of Wild Fauna and Flora (CITES), which serves as the primary vehicle for regulating wildlife trade. Foreign training and assistance programs to combat illegal wildlife trade are also conducted by some federal agencies, including the U.S. Department of State, which leads an international initiative against wildlife trafficking.

The role of Congress in evaluating U.S. policy to combat wildlife trafficking is broad. Potential issues for Congress include (1) determining funding levels for U.S. wildlife trade inspection and investigation; (2) evaluating the effectiveness of U.S. foreign aid to combat wildlife trafficking; (3) developing ways to encourage private-sector involvement in regulating the wildlife trade; (4) using trade sanctions to penalize foreign countries with weak enforcement of wildlife laws; (5) incorporating wildlife trade provisions into free trade agreements; and (6) addressing the domestic and international demand for illegal wildlife through public awareness campaigns and non-governmental organization partnerships. This report focuses on the international trade in terrestrial fauna, largely excluding trade in illegal plants, including timber, and fish.

BACKGROUND

Illegal wildlife trade involves the illicit procurement, transport, and distribution—internationally and domestically—of animals, and animal parts and derivatives thereof, in contravention of laws, foreign and domestic, and treaties. Illegal wildlife trade ranges in scale from single-item, local bartering to multi-ton, commercial-sized consignments shipped all over the world. Wildlife contraband may include live pets, hunting trophies, fashion accessories, cultural artifacts, ingredients for traditional medicines, wild meat for human consumption (or bushmeat), and other products.

Numerous reasons exist for wildlife trade regulation. Current international and domestic laws often seek to prevent (1) the decline of species threatened or potentially threatened with extinction; (2) the import of non-native species, which could harm the receiving habitats; (3) the import of species that could transmit diseases harmful to humans, animals, or plants; (4) the inhumane transport of wildlife; and (5) the distortion of trade in otherwise legitimate wildlife products, through unfair foreign pricing, government subsidies, and forms of illegal trade protectionism.

Congress has sought to regulate wildlife trade for more than a century, enacting the first wildlife trade prohibitions under the Lacey Act in 1900.[1] Congress also regulates wildlife trade under freestanding provisions in the Lacey Act Amendments of 1981, the Endangered Species Act of 1973, and other laws that prohibit the trade in specific threatened species or specific animals that pose potential health and disease risks.[2] (See *Appendix A*.) Internationally, wildlife trade is regulated to safeguard certain species threatened by over-exploitation and extinction. The primary international treaty governing wildlife trade is the United Nations Convention on International Trade in Endangered Species of Wild Fauna and Flora (CITES), which imposes an import- and export-control licensing system that restricts certain species from international trade.[3]

The primary motivation to engage in illegal wildlife trade appears to be economic gain. Continued demand in many parts of the world for illegal wildlife provides opportunities for criminals to turn profits along the supply chain. According to international law enforcement officials, some of the most lucrative illicit wildlife commodities include tiger parts, caviar, elephant ivory, rhino horn, and exotic birds and reptiles. Due to its clandestine nature, the illegal trade is difficult to quantify with any accuracy. Nevertheless, some estimate that it is worth at least $5 billion, and may potentially total in excess of $20 billion annually.[4] This would rank the illegal wildlife trade as among the most lucrative illicit economies in the world, behind illegal drugs and possibly human trafficking and arms trafficking.[5] According to the U.S. Department of State, the "illegal wildlife trade is often linked to organized crime and involves many of the same culprits and smuggling routes as trafficking in arms, drugs, and persons."[6]

The 111th Congress might address illegal wildlife crime through oversight hearings and legislation. Potential issues for Congress include (1) determining funding levels for U.S. wildlife trade inspection and investigation; (2) evaluating the effectiveness of U.S. foreign aid to combat wildlife trafficking; (3) developing ways to encourage private-sector involvement in regulating the wildlife trade; (4) using trade sanctions to penalize foreign countries with weak enforcement of wildlife laws; (5) incorporating wildlife trade provisions into free trade agreements; and (6) addressing the domestic and international demand for illegal wildlife through public awareness campaigns and non-governmental organization partnerships. This report focuses on the international trade in terrestrial fauna, largely excluding trade in illegal plants, including timber, and fish.

Demand

Global Demand

Demand for illegally obtained wildlife is ubiquitous. Some estimate that countries and regions with the highest demand for legally obtained wildlife include the United States, the People's Republic of China, and the European Union. Globally, demand for illegal wildlife is also increasing according to several observers. Some attribute this partly to increasing numbers of wildlife species regulated by CITES and other international and domestic wildlife protection laws.[7] Others caution that estimates of demand may be increasing because of greater public and governmental awareness of the issue in recent years, which has led to more investigations into the scope and magnitude of wildlife crime.[8] As a result, some analysts question whether demand for illegal wildlife is necessarily growing, or whether new data is simply capturing more information about a potentially stagnant or declining source of demand.

Reasons behind the current demand for illegal wildlife and related products appear to vary according to regions and cultures. In Asia, where analysts claim that a substantial portion— possibly the largest in the world—of the global trade of illegal wildlife takes place, demand is driven by the need for specific animal parts to practice traditional Asian medicine, for human consumption, and as symbols of wealth.[9] Demand for illegal wildlife is reportedly increasing in Southeast Asia due in part to the region's economic boom and resulting affluence.[10] In Africa, demand for illegal wildlife is driven by bushmeat consumption in rural and urban areas. In other regions, such as Europe and North America, analysts find that demand for illegal wildlife includes a wide variety of products, such as luxury fashion items, tourist souvenirs purchased abroad, and exotic pets, as well as traditional medicines and wildlife meats for human consumption.[11]

Quantifying U.S. Demand

While no reliable estimates of U.S. demand for illegal wildlife are publicly available, many analysts agree that demand for illegal wildlife in the

United States is likely to parallel U.S. demand for legal wildlife. If this is the case, the United States may be a significant destination for illegal wildlife, and the magnitude of the illegal trade may be increasing. The United States is estimated to purchase nearly 20% of all legal wildlife and wildlife products on the market.[12] Further, the value of U.S. legal wildlife trade has grown significantly in recent years—from $1.2 billion in FY2000 to $2.8 billion in FY2007.[13] (See *Table 1.)* In the same time period, the number of declared wildlife shipments has also grown—from 111,296 declared shipments in FY2000 to 179,323 in FY2007.[14] According to the U.S. Fish and Wildlife Service (FWS), which is the lead U.S. agency for wildlife trade law enforcement, illicit U.S. demand stems primarily from two sources: (1) wildlife items for personal use, such as tourist souvenirs or exotic pets, and (2) products for commercial use and products related to hunting (e.g., trophies).[15]

Table 1. Value of Legal Wildlife Imports and Refused Shipments into the United States, 2000-2007

Year	Value of Legal Trade[a]	Value of Refused Importsa	Percentage Illegal
2000	$1,200	$13.1	0.8%
2001	$1,800	$8.5	0.4%
2002	$1,500	$5.3	0.3%
2003	$1,700	$5.1	0.2%
2004	$1,900	$4.6	0.2%
2005	$2,300	n/a	n/a
2006	$2,200	n/a	n/a
2007	$2,800	n/a	n/a
2008	$2,800	n/a	n/a
2009	$2,700	n/a	n/a

Source: U.S. Department of the Interior, FWS, Office of Law Enforcement, Intelligence Unit, U.S. Illegal Wildlife

Trade: LEMIS Data Analysis and Risk Assessment, November 2005; and FWS response to CRS request January 29, 2010.

Note: n/a = not available.

[a] The value of illegal trade in wildlife given in this table reflects declared shipments that were refused entry at the U.S. border. It does not reflect the value of undetected wildlife shipments entering the United States, which may differ considerably from the values given in the table.

The globalization of trade and internationalization of the U.S. population and culture have apparently exacerbated the illegal wildlife trade. For example, immigrants from Central America have reportedly created a demand for sea turtle eggs and meat that cannot be met legally.[16] Further, reports indicate that demand for traditional Asian medicines, once confined to parts of Asia, has gained new users in the United States.[17]

Supply

Source countries of wildlife exports, both legal and illegal, tend to include countries across the developing world with rich biological diversity. Although definitive data are unavailable, many analysts argue that biologically rich countries with weak governance and poor law enforcement capacity may be especially vulnerable as sources for illegal wildlife trade.[18] While the United States is a source country for some wildlife including bears, predatory birds, and reptiles, most analysts indicate that U.S. wildlife is unlikely to play a large role in the illegal international market.

The United States, however, is a destination country for illegal wildlife products.

Table 2. Top 10 Countries from which Wildlife Imports Were Refused Entry into the United States, 2000-2004

Country	Shipments Refused Entry[a]
Mexico	3,772
Canada	1,560
People's Republic of China	1,138
Philippines	728
Hong Kong	591
Russia	562
Unknown[b]	524
Thailand	473
Italy	406
South Africa	341

Source: U.S. Department of Interior, FWS, Office of Law Enforcement, Intelligence Unit, U.S. Illegal Wildlife Trade: LEMIS Data Analysis and Risk Assessment, November 2005.

[a] Total refused shipments does not refer to the number of individual items to be shipped. As a result, the actual number of wildlife items shipped is substantially higher than indicated in this table.

[b] "Unknown" includes shipments found by FWS officials without packaging, labels, or supporting documentation showing the country of export.

According to a report published by FWS, the top three suppliers to the United States from which wildlife shipments were refused between 2000 and 2004, included Mexico, Canada, and the People's Republic of China.[19] (See *Table 2*.) These statistics, however, might be skewed because they are based only on shipments refused at the border and ignore undetected shipments.

Causes

Numerous factors explain the persistence of the international black market in wildlife. Observers suggest that one such factor is the high profits associated with wildlife trafficking. Driven by a demand for wildlife products that exceeds what the market can legally supply, the value of illegal wildlife products continues to increase as consumers are willing to pay greater amounts. (See *Table 3.)* Thus, as a certain type of animal or wildlife product becomes more endangered and rare, its price increases, along with the financial rewards for smugglers.[20]

Table 3. Selected Illicit Wildlife Trade and Estimated Retail Value

Illegally Traded Wildlife	Estimated Retail Value
Elephants	$121-$900 per kilogram of ivory
Rhinos	$945-$50,000 per kilogram of rhino horn
Tibetan Antelopes	$1,200-$20,000 per shatoosh shawl
Big Cats	$1,300-$20,000 per tiger, snow leopard, or jaguar skin; $3,300-$7,000 per set of tiger bones
Bears	$250-$8,500 per gallbladder
Sturgeon	$4,450-$6,000 per kilogram of caviar
Reptiles and Insects (often live)	$30,000 per oenpelli python; $30,000 per komodo dragon; $5,000-$30,000 per plowshare tortoise; $15,000 per Chinese alligator; $20,000 per monitor lizard; $20,000 per shingleback skink; $8,500 per pair of birdwing butterflies
Exotic Birds (often live)	$10,000 per black palm cockatoo egg ($25,000-$80,000 per mature breeding pair); $5,000-$12,000 per hyacinth macaw; $60,000-$90,000 per lear macaw; $20,000 per Mongolian falcon
Great Apes (often live)	$50,000 per Orangutan

Sources: Compiled from U.S. government agencies, international organizations, non-governmental organizations, and media sources.

In many developing countries, however, the income derived from illegal wildlife poaching and trading is often vital for sustaining the livelihoods of impoverished hunters and traders. Some observers say small-scale hunters and traders have few alternatives for generating subsistence-level incomes.[21] Additionally, some indigenous peoples may consider hunting certain animals a fundamental part of their culture, religion, or traditions. These considerations may differentiate poor hunters and traders from international criminal syndicates involved in the trade, who engage in the trade purely for profit.

Another factor is the perceived low risk of capture or penalties associated with wildlife trafficking.[22] Such a perception can be the consequence of limited enforcement capabilities or willingness to punish such illegal behavior, due to a lack of resources, infrastructure, expertise, or political corruption. Additionally, the wildlife trade may be considered less risky than other high-value black markets, including the drug trade, as the penalties associated with wildlife crime tend to be substantially less severe than with other trafficking crimes. According to a series of United Nations reports, powdered rhinoceros horn can be worth more than the equivalent weight of cocaine or gold. Combined with the "low level of vigilance" and "modest level of penalties" applied to wildlife crime cases, criminal entrepreneurs are attracted by the prospect of high profits and low risks.[23]

Pathways

Illicit wildlife trade uses complex distribution networks connecting raw material from source states and producers of wildlife products to customers.[24] Observers have yet to identify a distinct criminal profile that describes wildlife poachers and traffickers.[25] Illicit wildlife trade networks can involve a combination of any of the following: (1) village hunters, who trade small wildlife as a source of subsistence cash income or who kill some wildlife to protect their people and crops from attacks; (2) wildlife experts; (3) criminal entities, sometimes including terrorists, rebels, drug traffickers, and others, able to evade detection, and transport and secure the products, as well as launder the proceeds; (4) legitimate businesses serving as a front for the trade; (5) corrupt government officials to facilitate import and export; and (6) consumers willing to pay for the contraband.

Various combinations of these actors conspire to exploit a variety of trafficking pathways, which appear to be growing as globalization has improved the ease of travel, transport, transactions, and other cross-border barriers that previously limited wildlife trade. The magnitude of highly organized criminal syndicates' role in wildlife trafficking is subject to debate. Although little is certain about wildlife traffickers, anecdotal evidence indicates that suppliers have historically tended to work in small, but well-organized groups.[26] Organized criminal syndicates, by contrast, while likely to be participating in the trade of certain, high-value wildlife commodities—including caviar, traditional Asian medicine, ivory, and reptile skins—are not necessarily operating in all segments of the illegal wildlife trade.[27]

Some observers, including officials from FWS and Interpol, have identified a growth in the scope, sophistication, and organization of wildlife crime in recent years. According to one FWS report, investigations increasingly involve "multiple suspects in multiple locations committing multiple felonies."[28] Traffickers are reportedly connected globally to suppliers of exotic animals in developing countries; consumers at upscale art galleries; safari operators guiding hunters to illegal animal trophies; and international and interstate networks of wildlife exporters, taxidermists, and wildlife retailers.

In the process of trafficking live animals and wildlife products, contents are often smuggled through three primary methods: (1) hidden in secret compartments of luggage, shipping containers, or clothing; (2) mis-declared on customs forms and trade permits by fraudulently identifying look-alike, non-protected species, changing the declared number of items shipped, changing the declared value of items, or declaring wild species as captive-bred species; or (3) trafficked using forged or stolen trade permits to give the false impression that the contents are being legitimately traded.[29] In other cases, observers have also found live animals and wildlife products trafficked using common delivery services (e.g. postal services, Fedex, DHL, and others) as well as diplomatic luggage not subject to scrutiny. Additional potential areas of market growth include the Internet, where traders are reportedly using chat rooms and auction websites, such as eBay, to engage in illicit wildlife sales.[30]

Case Study: Tracing the African Ivory Trade

The African elephant population has dwindled from roughly 1.2 million in the 1970s to less than 500,000 today.[31] In 1989, CITES effectively banned international, commercial elephant ivory trade; most trade in elephant ivory today remains illegal.[32] Widely hailed as a success by many observers, the 1989 ban resulted in a near-disappearance of the illegal elephant ivory market. In the past several years, however, many analysts are concerned that the trade has rekindled— primarily driven by a surging demand for ivory jewelry, or other symbols of wealth in Japan, the People's Republic of China, and several other countries in Asia. Between August 2005 and August 2006, authorities across the world seized more than 26 metric tons of illegally trafficked elephant ivory.[33] In October 2009, TRAFFIC, a non-governmental organization that monitors wildlife trade issues, released an analysis of ivory seizure data based on the Elephant Trade Information System (ETIS). The report concluded that the illicit trade in elephant ivory has been increasing in volume since 2004 and surged in particular in 2009.[34]

The price of wholesale elephant ivory has reportedly skyrocketed from approximately $100 per kilogram in the late 1990s, to $200 per kilogram by 2004, to as much as $900 per kilogram today.[35] Based on a TRAFFIC study of 12,400 elephant ivory tusk seizures since the ivory ban, seizures are growing in both frequency and size.[36] On average, there are reportedly three seizures of ivory tusks each day worldwide, which can range in scale from a few tourist trinkets to six-ton, commercial consignments. Many observers suggest that the larger, commercial-sized shipments often use sophisticated means to evade law enforcement authorities.

Experts generally contend that elephants from central Africa are the primary targets of poachers today, with additional poaching hotspots surfacing around Zimbabwe, Tanzania, and Zambia.[37]

Based on an analysis of elephant product seizure data from 1998 to 2006, the most heavily implicated ivory trading countries include Cameroon, the People's Republic of China, the Democratic Republic of Congo, and Nigeria.[38] U.S. and international law enforcement officials also indicate that highly organized cross-border poachers from Sudan and Somalia are poaching elephant populations in Chad and Kenya.[39] Analysts suspect that large-scale ivory trafficking involves transnational crime syndicates, which are located in African source countries and along transit routes through countries that include Tanzania, Djibouti, United Arab Emirates, Hong Kong, Macao, Philippines, and Singapore.[40]

Due to the clandestine nature of the activity, analysts have difficulty identifying specific pathways of illicit wildlife trade. However, one documented case of elephant ivory trafficking, which law enforcement officials clandestinely monitored, provides some insight into how the illicit trade in African elephant ivory operates. This case also highlights the often circuitous pathways that illicit shipments travel to avoid detection: In 2006, Taiwanese authorities confiscated more than five metric tons of elephant ivory over a three-day period, concealed in shipping cargo. Shipping documents indicated that the illegal consignment originated in Tanzania and was destined for the Philippines. After departing from Tanzania, the ivory transited through Malaysia and into Singapore, where the cargo remained for some time. The shipment then departed for the Philippines but was re-routed to Taiwan. From Taiwan, the consignment arrived in the Philippines, but, without being offloaded, returned to Taiwan. As the ivory was about to return to the Philippines—with shipping documents identifying a different importer than when the shipment was originally sent to the Philippines—Taiwanese authorities confiscated the contraband. Shortly after the seizure, however, the five tons of ivory disappeared from a storage warehouse contracted by Philippine customs authorities while the case remained under further investigation.[41]

In November 2009, U.S. and Thai officials announced the results of a separate, two year-long joint investigation involving an alleged transnational African ivory smuggling operation. To date, the investigation has resulted in the U.S. indictment of two individuals and four criminal arrests.[42]

THREATS

Environmental Implications

The illegal wildlife trade can affect the natural resources and environment of importing and exporting countries. The potential environmental harm of the illegal wildlife trade include (1) reducing biodiversity, (2) disrupting ecosystems by introducing non-native species, and (3) and transmitting disease.

Threats to Biodiversity

Observers report that the illegal wildlife trade may directly contribute to the decline of some species. In addition, others report that the illegal wildlife trade combines with habitat loss or alteration to contribute to species decline. The actual extinction of species as a result solely of trade is not widely documented in the literature,[43] although exploitation combined with habitat loss and alteration, is linked to significant declines in several species.[44] Some observers, for example, claim that while great apes make up less than 1% of the bushmeat trade in West and Central Africa, this rate of harvest, combined with habitat loss and alteration, has led to very severe population declines; if this trend is unchecked, extinction is likely.[45] Species that are currently in decline due primarily to exploitation for trade are species that are rare or have historically low population levels. For example, some have attributed sharp declines in three rare species of tropical Asian bears to the illegal trade in bear parts, especially bear gallbladders, for use in traditional Asian medicine.[46]

Insufficient data and a lack of understanding of how the trade affects wildlife populations limit current knowledge of the impact of illegal wildlife trade on biodiversity. A study seeking to measure the impact of the trade on wild populations of amphibians and reptiles, for example, was inconclusive because the authors were unable to obtain comprehensive data on the actual amount of wildlife traded through licit and illicit channels, as well as the sustainable harvest rate of species in the wild.[47] Further, research remains incomplete in understanding how illegal wildlife trade could indirectly affect ecosystems, when species important to the functioning of the ecosystem are depleted. Some analysts suggest that the illegal harvesting of wildlife could indirectly affect ecosystems when species important to the functioning of the ecosystem are reduced.[48]

Invasive Species[49]

Illegal wildlife trade may introduce harmful, non-native species that could disrupt ecosystems. Non-native species can affect human, animal, and plant health, causing considerable economic and environmental damage.[50] Many non-native species that were introduced to the United States came initially through legal channels, some of them through the pet trade.[51] Such species are often banned from import only after government officials find documented evidence of a nonnative species' threat to humans, agriculture, or ecosystems.[52] Some banned species, however, still enter the country illegally through trade. Chinese mitten crabs, for example, banned under the Lacey Act, continue to be smuggled into the United States and Europe for consumption. Chinese mitten crabs are harmful to the environment if released; they damage riverbanks by their burrowing and clog drainage systems.

The impact of non-native species is also considered a contributing factor for listing indigenous species as endangered or threatened. Congress identified non-native species as the second-leading contributing factor, after habitat loss and alteration, for listings under the Endangered Species Act of 1973, affecting nearly half of all threatened and endangered native species.[53] Non-native species may out-compete native species for prey, transmit diseases to native species, and alter native ecosystems. For example, the Burmese python is a non-native species brought illegally from Southeast Asia to parts of the United States as a pet.[54] These pythons consume large quantities of native prey and compete with alligators at the top of the food chain.[55] The entry of non-native species is reportedly increasing in the United States and globally. In San

Francisco Bay, a new non-native species now enters the ecosystem every 14 weeks, on average, compared to an average of one every 55 weeks from 1851 to 1960.[56]

Disease

Another concern includes the potential entry and spread of animal-borne diseases through the illegal trade in wildlife.[57] According to some, the ability of human and other diseases to spread throughout the world is becoming increasingly linked to the global nature of wildlife trade, coupled with the expansion of regional and international transportation routes.[58] Diseases transmitted through wildlife may affect not only humans and result in outbreaks that cause social and economic harm, but also threaten native wildlife and ecosystems.[59] Indeed, some have stated that the most dangerous emerging infectious diseases, in terms of total fatalities and fatality rates, have come from wildlife.[60] According to the General Accounting Office (now Government Accountability Office), nearly 75% of emerging diseases reach humans through animals.[61] The link between the illegal wildlife trade and disease, however, remains contested by some analysts as being mostly an unrealized threat. Indeed, little is known about the extent to which illegally imported wildlife may carry harmful diseases.[62]

Several countries have reported disease outbreaks caused by wildlife trade. However, most documented disease outbreaks linked to wildlife trade involve imports and exports of legal wildlife. After an outbreak, the suspected wildlife might be banned from import, effectively making its trade illegal in the affected country. In the United States, diseases from imported wildlife have infected or threaten native species, livestock, and humans. Some examples include the following:

- *Severe Acute Respiratory Syndrome (SARS):* The SARS virus can infect wildlife and humans. Experts suspect that SARS originated in the People's Republic of China, where SARS-infected civets, a variety of wild cat common in the Chinese wildlife trade, came in contact with humans.[63] Although civets remain legally traded in China, the Centers for Disease Control and Prevention (CDC) banned civet imports into the United States.
- *Heartwater Disease:* Heartwater is a disease of cattle, sheep, and goats, and can cause mortality rates of 60% in cattle and up to 100% in sheep.[64] African tortoise ticks that reside on some imported snakes and tortoises carry this disease. The U.S. Department of Agriculture

(USDA) banned the import and interstate commerce of three types of African tortoises because African ticks carrying heartwater were found on them.

- *Avian Influenza:* Highly pathogenic avian influenza virus (H5N1) can infect humans through poultry-human interactions. Its natural reservoir is wild birds, but it can be transmitted through poultry as well. Avian flu has been common in live bird markets and can be disseminated through wildlife trade.[65] CDC has banned poultry and poultry products from bird flu source countries.
- *Monkeypox:* Monkeypox infects wildlife commonly found in Africa, and can spread to wildlife native to the United States and humans. Monkeypox was introduced to the United States by legally imported African rodents. The rodents transmitted the disease to prairie dogs in a pet store. The prairie dogs were, in turn, the source for transmitting the disease to humans.[66] CDC has banned all African rodents from entering the United States, except under certain circumstances.

Some have suggested that since many diseases are zoonotic (diseases that can be passed from animals to humans), the wildlife trade might have bio-terrorism implications. For example, imports of lightly regulated wildlife might be used to carry a disease that could be transmitted to other animals or agricultural crops. Another possibility might be intentionally importing and releasing ill animals to spread a disease to humans. Zoonotic diseases, included plague, tularemia, and hantavirus, have been used in weapons programs.[67] The Japanese during the 1930s, for example, used fleas to cause plague in China.[68] Some have suggested that a terrorist group with access to pathogens, but lacking dissemination technology, could conceivably use animal vectors to transmit the disease.[69] However, no open source evidence is currently available to suggests that terrorists are planning attacks involving the transmission of disease through illegal wildlife trade.

Congress is addressing zoonotic disease transmission through proposed legislation that would add non-human primates (e.g., chimpanzees and apes) to the list of prohibited wildlife species under the Lacey Act (H.R. 80).[70] This legislation is directed toward the non-human primate pet trade and would make it illegal to import, export, transport, sell, receive, acquire, or purchase (in interstate or foreign commerce) non-human primates with exceptions (e.g., for science and zoos). It would not make it illegal to possess a non-human primate. Some who support this legislation cite the propensity of non-human primates to transmit disease to, and inflict injury on humans and animals.[71]

Some others who oppose this legislation contend that non-human primates kept as pets in the United States generally do not carry disease and should not be considered a threat to the safety of others.[72]

Case Study: Illegal Bushmeat Trade

Illegal bushmeat trade refers to the harvesting of wildlife for consumption and its subsequent trafficking within or outside source countries.[73] Although many cultures around the world consume wildlife meat, the term bushmeat commonly refers to wildlife hunted in African forests. Bushmeat trade is considered illegal when imports occur in contravention of CITES, national quarantine laws, and other laws than ban the trade of specific animals.[74] In Africa, this illegal trade is considered a threat to the diversity and abundance of endangered and threatened animal species, and the ecosystems in which they reside. Some are also concerned that illegal bushmeat trade could facilitate the transmission of exotic diseases throughout the world.

Illegal bushmeat trade in Africa is driven primarily by economic gain and subsistence, and is greatest in areas of West and Central Africa. The illegal bushmeat trade is reportedly a significant, and sometimes primary, source of income in Africa, generating an estimated $50 million annually.[75] The bushmeat trade is a significant source of protein for many communities in Africa, especially among the rural poor. Bushmeat provides an affordable source of animal protein as well as income-generating opportunities.[76] In some cases, bushmeat is preferred over domestic sources of meat by Africans. It is estimated that between 1 and 3.4 million tons of bushmeat are consumed annually in Africa, of which 60% is consumed in urban centers, where demand is highest.[77] Further, illegal bushmeat is sold primarily in urban markets in some parts of Africa, where they generate greater profits than legal bushmeat.[78] The illegal bushmeat trade also satisfies a global demand, which includes certain communities in the United States.

Entry of bushmeat into the United States is a concern because of its potential to carry disease.[79] This concern is exacerbated because the health of the animal from which the bushmeat is derived is not documented and the meat is generally not screened for diseases at the border.[80] Bushmeat is associated with several diseases that affect humans. The United States has experienced outbreaks from diseases such as HIV/AIDS, which some suggest emerged in Africa through consuming primates that carry the Simian Immunodeficiency Viruses (SIV);[81] and monkeypox, which originated from African rodents, commonly consumed as bushmeat and traded globally. Other diseases that affect humans and are linked to bushmeat include the Ebola hemorrhagic fever, which has been transmitted to bushmeat hunters who were in contact with infected great apes; and the SARS coronavirus, which has been associated with the international trade in small carnivores.[82]

CDC bans imports of certain animals, including African rodents, known to be prominent in bushmeat trade and vectors of disease.[83] In response to avian influenza, CDC and USDA banned imports of birds and unprocessed bird products from countries with the avian flu virus in domestic poultry. Other species that are known to carry diseases (e.g., non-human primates and live bats) may require a permit from CDC and other agencies for import into the United States.

Security Implications

The impact of wildlife smuggling has the potential to reach beyond environmental threats. Numerous sources indicate that organized criminal syndicates, insurgency groups, and military units are among the primary actors involved in large-scale, commercial-sized wildlife trafficking. Limited anecdotal evidence also indicates that some terrorist groups may be engaged in the wildlife smuggling trade for monetary gain. Some observers claim that the participation of such actors in wildlife trafficking can threaten the stability of countries, foster corruption, and encourage the use of violence to protect the trade.[84]

Links to Organized Crime

According to a series of U.N. studies on the illicit traffic of wildlife, wildlife experts claim that Chinese, Japanese, Italian, and Russian organized crime syndicates are "heavily involved in illegal wildlife trade."[85] While such claims do not suggest that organized crime syndicates are involved in all forms of wildlife trafficking, the United Nations reports that syndicates are "strongly present" in some sectors. Further, even when criminal syndicates are not controlling the trade, much of the trafficking is commonly described as "highly organized."[86]

East Asian Triad societies, such as the Wo Shing Wo group and 14K, as well as the Japanese Yakuza, have reportedly smuggled elephant ivory, rhino horn, tigers, shark fin, abalone, and whale meat.[87] The United Nations also reports that "no sector of the illegal fauna and flora trade has been criminalized to the extent of that of sturgeon and caviar." Most of the caviar business is reportedly controlled by Russian organized crime, which several analysts also claim is engaged in the poaching of tigers and bears.[88] According to FWS, recent investigations into U.S. caviar trade revealed that seven of the ten major importers on the East Coast had been illegally importing millions of dollars worth of caviar annually.[89]

Members of the Italian Mafia, the former Medellin drug cartel in Colombia, and possibly additional groups in Central Asia and Brazil reportedly have been involved in the illicit trafficking of rare parrots or falcons.[90] Anecdotal accounts also indicate that some organized groups are involved in both illegal wildlife and human trafficking.[91]

Links to Drug Trafficking

A 2002 British study, commissioned by the World Wildlife Fund and the World Conservation Union, found that key illicit drug production and distribution countries that coincide with major source states for endangered wildlife are areas where illicit wildlife trafficking has likely taken place.[92] Anecdotal evidence indicates that illicit wildlife has been found to be smuggled along the same routes as narcotics as a subsidiary trade for drug traffickers, especially in Latin America. The United Nations reports that members of the former Cali drug cartel in Colombia and Mexican drug dealers have also allegedly smuggled mixed shipments of drugs and wildlife products into the United States.[93]

According to the Brazilian National Network Against the Trafficking of Wild Animals (RENCTAS), 40% of an estimated 400 criminal rings smuggling animals were also involved in other criminal activities, especially drug trafficking.[94] The CITES Secretariat has also reported that combinations of parrots and drugs have been smuggled together from Cote d'Ivoire to Israel.[95]

Wildlife, both legal and illegal, are also used as the means to conceal illegal drugs. In one famous case, U.S. Customs Service inspectors in Miami recovered 86 pounds of cocaine-filled condoms from Colombia, which had been inserted into 225 boa constrictor snakes.[96] More recently, international law enforcement officials say they have confiscated mixes of narcotics and illicit wildlife that range from elephant tusks with hashish stuffed inside to exotic birds smuggled with methamphetamine pills.[97] Wildlife products are reportedly also used as a currency in exchange for drugs. According to FWS officials, smugglers often trade illegal drugs for endangered animals in cashless transfers that serve as a special form of money laundering. In South Africa, street gangs reportedly provide highly prized, but illegal, catches of abalone to Asian crime syndicates for methamphetamine.[98]

Links to Terrorism

There is limited publicly available evidence of terrorist groups involved in wildlife trafficking.

According to U.N. reports and Interpol officials, some insurgent groups and possibly terrorist groups are reportedly engaged in illegal poaching for profit in several areas of Asia and Africa.[99]

The limited anecdotal evidence indicates that terrorist groups may be engaged in illegal wildlife smuggling for monetary gain, if sources of rich biodiversity are near their operating arenas. *Figure 1* shows noted regions of high biodiversity and their proximity to selected zones of possible terrorist safe havens.[100]

Although not necessarily indicative of an existing relationship between terrorists and wildlife trafficking, the map highlights the possibility of terrorist groups or other criminal entities in regions of high biodiversity taking advantage of porous borders, weak states, and criminal sympathizers.

Some experts caution that terrorist involvement may be more of an exception to the overall scope of wildlife trafficking, rather than indicative of an emerging trend or pervasive characteristic of illegal wildlife trade. Other experts suggest that terrorist groups may look to organized crime groups, some of which are known to traffic in illegal wildlife, as models for financing terrorist activities.[101]

Both types of groups benefit from generating clandestine sources of income in nonlegal markets. Al Qaeda, for example, has been allegedly involved in several forms of organized crime, such as money laundering and credit card fraud, to fund its activities.[102] Some experts also suggest that the loosely-connected, cellular structure of some international terrorist organizations today may lend itself to increased links between terrorism and organized crime.

Experts argue that as loosely connected terrorist cells are expected to secure their own funding, organized crime may present itself as an attractive funding option.[103]

Some law enforcement officials indicate that Somali elephant and rhino poachers are now linked to at least one Somali warlord, who has provided safe haven and other forms of protection to known Al Qaeda operatives.[104] In Kaziranga, India, two Islamic extremist groups with ties to Al Qaeda, Harakat ul-Jihad-I-Islami/Bangladesh (HUJI-B) and Jamaatul Mujahedin Bangladesh (JMB), are reportedly sponsoring elephant and rhino poaching for profit, according to several news articles.[105]

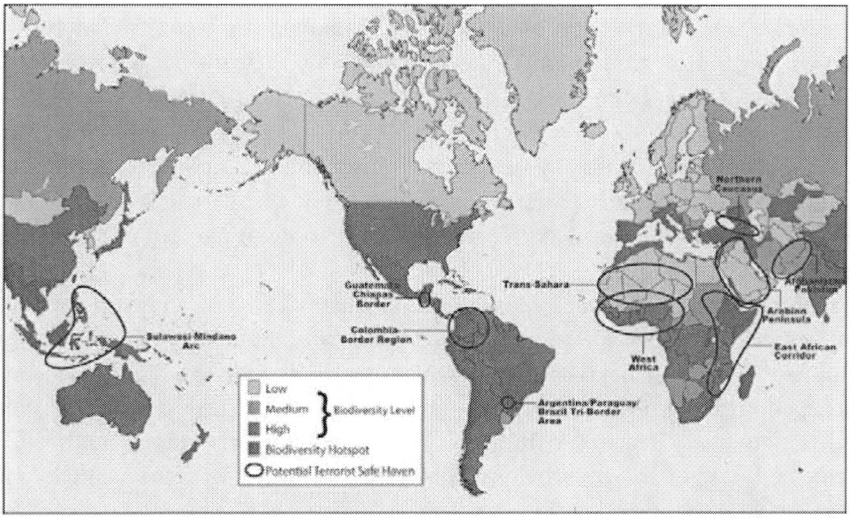

Sources: For "Potential Terrorist Safe Haven": U.S. Department of State, Office of the Coordinator for Terrorism, Country Reports on Terrorism, Chapter 5: Terrorist Safe Havens, April 2007; and Angel Rabasa et al., Ungoverned Territories: Understanding and Reducing Terrorism Risks (Santa Monica, CA: Rand Corporation, 2007). For "Biodiversity Level": Brian Groombridge and Martin D. Jenkins, World Atlas of Biodiversity (Berkeley, CA: University of California Press, 2002). For "Biodiversity Hotspot": Conservation International, Biodiversity Hotspots, at http://www.biodiversityhotspots.org, accessed February 19, 2008.

Note: This map does not imply that terrorists are necessarily involved in wildlife trafficking where zones of high biodiversity and potential safe havens overlap. Additionally, it should be noted that the State Department and the Rand Corporation data differs on which regions are potential safe havens. Actual and potential locations identified by the State Department include Somalia; the Trans-Sahara, including Mali, Mauritania, Niger, Algeria, and Chad; the Sulu/Sulawesi Seas Littoral, including the southern Philippines and Indonesia; Iraq, including northern Iraq; Lebanon; Yemen; Afghanistan and Pakistan, including the Afghanistan-Pakistan border; the Colombia border region; and the Tri-Border area, including Argentina, Brazil, and Paraguay. Locations identified by Rand include the Pakistan-Afghanistan border, the Arabian Peninsula, the Sulawesi-Mindano arc, East Africa, West Africa, the Northern Caucasus, the Colombia-Venezuela border, and the Guatemala-Chiapas border.

Figure 1. Regions of Biodiversity and Selected Terrorist Safe Havens.

Links to Weak States and Political Instability

Wildlife criminals may seek to exploit countries with a weak capacity to govern, poor law enforcement, high government corruption, and porous borders.[106] These country characteristics, common to weak states in the developing world, are not only frequently linked to drug trafficking, organized crime, and, on occasion, terrorism, but are also reportedly linked to the illegal trade in wildlife.

Analysts contend that weak states at any point along wildlife trafficking routes—source countries, transit countries, and destination countries—are especially attractive to wildlife criminals, who hope to operate in these countries with impunity.

For example, several reports indicate that weak law enforcement and uncontrolled borders in Southeast Asia—especially the border region between Burma, Thailand, China, and Laos, which is also known as a significant drug production and trafficking region—are contributing to the problem.[107] Sun bears, clouded leopards, Burmese pythons, monitor lizards, and other protected species are reportedly available for sale in numerous markets and trading posts throughout Southeast Asia.

According to some observers, the lack of law enforcement along these borders is contributing to the local extinction of several wildlife species.[108]

In rare instances, extensive cross-border, commercial poaching and trafficking operations have reportedly been associated with political instability in certain regions.

This has been documented in several cases in Africa, where some conflicts have been reportedly financed, in part, by the elephant ivory trade. As local elephant populations decline, Sudanese and Somalis have also been known to stage heavily-armed ivory raids across their borders into Kenya, Chad, and the Central African Republic—using machine guns, rocket launchers, and other sophisticated weapons not only to poach wildlife but to fight park rangers and other border guards they may encounter.

Rebel groups from Sudan, for example, would reportedly trade elephant ivory, sometimes dubbed "conflict ivory," for military weapons, and Somali troops were once reportedly encouraged to poach ivory in lieu of receiving salaries.[109] According to discussions with law enforcement officials and media reports, members of the Sudanese Janjaweed militia are also poaching elephants in and around Chad's Zakouma National Park.[110]

Other militia or insurgent groups that were allegedly involved in wildlife trafficking for profit include Mozambique's Mozambican National Resistance (RENAMO) and Angola's National Union for the Total Independence of Angola (UNITA).[111]

U.S. Policy

Law Enforcement and Trade Inspection

Several agencies are responsible for law enforcement and trade inspection involving wildlife trade, including the Department of Homeland Security's Customs and Border Patrol (CBP) and the Department of the Interior's Fish and Wildlife Service (FWS). CBP maintains the primary authority to inspect goods imported into the United States and vessels carrying goods into U.S. ports of entry. If wildlife goods are declared they are generally referred to FWS, which is the primary agency responsible for inspecting wildlife shipments. Other agencies also have some authorities to inspect wildlife trade, including the Department of Commerce's National Oceanic and Atmospheric Administration (NOAA), the Department of Agriculture's Animal and Plant Health Inspection Service (APHIS), and the Department of Health and Human Services' Centers for Disease Control and Prevention (CDC). Inspectors from these agencies may not be trained to handle all types of wildlife imports; as a result, when inspectors from one agency need guidance or clarification on a shipment, other relevant agencies are contacted.

Fish and Wildlife Service

FWS is responsible for monitoring and detecting illegal trade in endangered species, invasive species, and other statutorily regulated wildlife. Under the Endangered Species Act of 1973 and the Lacey Act and Lacey Act Amendments of 1981, FWS has the authority to detain and inspect any international shipment of wildlife, including items in baggage, parcels, or vehicles. In 2007, FWS posted 114 uniformed wildlife inspectors at 38 ports of entry across the country—at 18 designated ports, through which most wildlife traffic is required to pass, border ports, and a handful of other ports.[112] (See *Figure 2*.) Ports are designated for importing and exporting wildlife to consolidate shipments for inspectors. Under certain circumstances, some wildlife shipments may travel through non-designated ports.[113] A designated port, however, must be used for importing wildlife that requires a permit under certain federal regulations that cover threatened and endangered species, marine mammals, and CITES listed species, among others. See *Table 4* for changes in the quantity and activity of FWS inspectors from 2000 to 2006.

FWS reportedly inspects approximately 25% of declared wildlife shipments at the U.S. border.[114] FWS does not inspect undeclared shipments except during planned investigations or seasonal periods when certain illegally obtained wildlife have a higher probability of being imported into the United States. Undeclared shipments may also be targeted for inspection if FWS has reason to suspect that the shipment could be contraband. Shipments containing wildlife that are in transit through the United States are generally not required to be declared to FWS. However, in-transit shipments must comply with foreign and domestic wildlife laws, including the humane transport of live animals. Certain species listed on endangered or threatened species lists under the Endangered Species Act of 1973, migratory birds, marine mammals, or injurious species listed under the Lacey Act and Lacey Act Amendments of 1981, among others, may not transit within the United States.

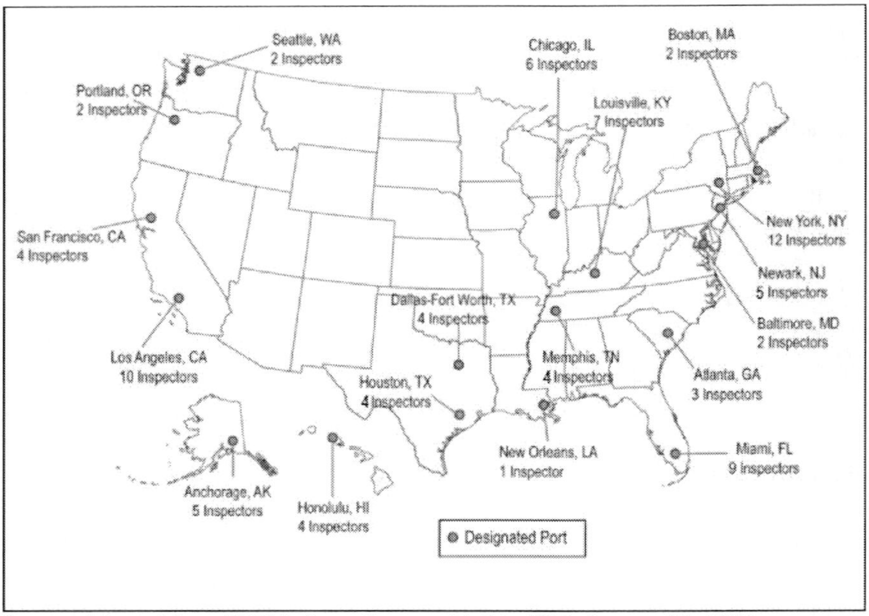

Source: Adapted from FWS information provided to CRS, January 29, 2010.

Figure 2. Map of FWS Designated Ports and Number of Inspectors.

Customs and Border Control

CBP's mission is to protect U.S. borders from terrorism, human and drug smuggling, illegal migration, and agricultural pests while facilitating the flow of legitimate travel and trade. CBP addresses the illegal wildlife trade directly by preventing the entry of exotic plant and animal pests, and any other emerging threats in agro- and bio-terrorism from entering the country.

Table 4. Statistics on the Activities of the U.S. Fish and Wildlife Office of Law Enforcement

Year	FWS Office of Law Enforcement Enacted Budget (in constant U.S. millions)	Number of Special Agents[a]	Number of Wildlife Inspectors[a]	Investigative Caseload	Number of Declared Shipments[b]	Number of Staffed Ports of Entry
FY2000	$48.1	201	90	9,105	111,296	29
FY2001	$59.2	224	90	8,681	120,004	30
FY2002	$39.2	238	88	8,412	123,720	30
FY2003	$59.4	229	94	10,369	139,541	31
FY2004	$60.1	231	95	10,536	157,617	31
FY2005	$60.4	218	105	13,980	172,404	35
FY2006	$58.7	202	112	15,128	183,247	38
FY2007	$57.3	199	114	12,177	187,670	37
FY2008	$59.6	201	117	14,933	186,959	37
FY2009	$62.7	195	116	13,097	169,728[c]	37
Avg. annual % change, FY2000-FY2009	5.2%	-0.2%	2.9%	5.4%[d]	5.0%	2.9%

Source: FWS, Office of Law Enforcement, Annual Reports, FY2000-FY2007, at http://www.fws.gov/le/AboutLE/ annual.htm, visited February 2, 2009; FWS response to CRS request, January 29, 2010.

[a] Number lists end-of-year size of forces.

[b] The number of declared shipments does not reflect the actual number of individual items traded. For example, a shipment with 1,000 geckos or 10 geckos would be counted as one shipment. In addition, this statistic does not take into account the amount of wildlife trade that is not declared to U.S. officials. As a result, the number of wildlife items shipped per year is likely to be higher than indicated in this table.

[c] Shipment total for FY2009 may increase as additional data entry continues.

[d] Note that from 2000 to 2006 there was nearly a 10% average annual increase per year in caseloads. It is unclear what caused the nearly 20% caseload reduction from 2006 to 2007.

CBP collaborates with other agencies, including FWS, when they find suspicious wildlife shipments. CBP is also considered by U.S. officials as the first line of defense against import of undeclared illegal wildlife shipments.

Customs and Border Control

CBP's mission is to protect U.S. borders from terrorism, human and drug smuggling, illegal migration, and agricultural pests while facilitating the flow of legitimate travel and trade. CBP addresses the illegal wildlife trade directly by preventing the entry of exotic plant and animal pests, and any other emerging threats in agro- and bio-terrorism from entering the country. CBP collaborates with other agencies, including FWS, when they find suspicious wildlife shipments. CBP is also considered by U.S. officials as the first line of defense against import of undeclared illegal wildlife shipments.

Animal and Plant Health Inspection Service

The U.S. Department of Agriculture's APHIS regulates the imports of some animal and animal products that could harm agriculture or livestock. Among its responsibilities, APHIS serves to facilitate safe international trade, monitor the health of animals presented at the border, and regulate the import and export of animals and animal products. APHIS enforces provisions of the Animal Health Protection Act,[115] which give APHIS the authority to prohibit or restrict the importation of any animal if it will prevent a pest or disease from affecting agriculture or livestock. Further, APHIS has the authority to prosecute individuals who smuggle any animals or animal products into the country. APHIS works with FWS and CBP to monitor agricultural imports at the border and has a dedicated team for investigating the illegal wildlife trade.[116]

In response to the growing volume of smuggled and improperly imported agricultural products entering the United States, APHIS created the Smuggling Intervention and Trade Compliance unit (SITC), a special anti-smuggling unit to prevent the unlawful entry and distribution of prohibited agricultural commodities, and products that may harbor harmful wildlife, including animal pests, diseases, and invasive species.[117] The unit routinely works with CBP agents during agricultural anti-smuggling and cooperative interdiction efforts at air, land, and sea ports of entry.

National Oceanic and Atmospheric Administration

NOAA's National Marine Fisheries Service (NMFS) enforces laws that protect and regulate the marine resources of the United States. Some of these laws, such as the Magnuson-Stevens Fishery Conservation and Management Act, regulate the trade and catch of marine organisms.[118] NOAA Fisheries Service also enforces trade in CITES-regulated marine species. NOAA's Office of Law Enforcement uses special agents to patrol the sea, conduct investigations, monitor fishing practices, inspect fish processing plants, and review sales of wildlife products on the Internet. Some agents are also stationed at the border to assist in the inspection of imports.

Centers for Disease Control and Prevention

The Department of Health and Human Services' CDC takes the lead in protection against communicable human diseases at the border. In recent years, CDC has banned certain wildlife imports to prevent the introduction, transmission, and spread into the United States of specific diseases from animals to humans, including monkeypox (African rodents), SARS (civets), and the highly pathogenic avian influenza H5N1 (birds and bird products from source countries).[119] Under its delegated authority, CDC's Division of Global Migration and Quarantine is empowered to detain, medically examine, or conditionally release individuals and wildlife suspected of carrying a communicable disease. Not all diseases are quarantinable; zoonotic diseases that are, however, include SARS and influenza, such as bird flu, that is causing or has the potential to cause a pandemic.[120] CDC officials are not present at the border on a day-to-day basis, but maintain quarantine stations located in Anchorage, Atlanta, Boston, Chicago, Dallas, Detroit, El Paso, Honolulu, Houston, Los Angeles, Miami, Minneapolis, New York, Newark, Philadelphia, San Diego, San Francisco, San Juan, Seattle, and Washington, D.C.

Wildlife Crime Prosecution

The Department of Justice (DOJ) prosecutes individuals and organizations charged with wildlife trafficking. The Environment and Natural Resources Division (ENRD), within DOJ, is responsible for all environmental and natural resources-related litigation, including wildlife crimes, filed on behalf of or against the United States in federal courts.[121] Investigations initiated by law enforcement agents from FWS, NOAA, and other agencies related to the illegal wildlife trade are referred to ENRD for prosecution.

Wildlife traffickers face charges from traditional wildlife trafficking statutes such as the Lacey Act and the Endangered Species Act, but also from other statutes that prohibit money laundering, smuggling, and conspiracy.[122] One of the primary statutes for prosecuting wildlife traffickers is the Lacey Act and Lacey Act Amendments of 1981, which prohibits the (1) import, export, transport, selling, receiving, acquiring, or purchase of any fish or wildlife already taken, possessed, transported, or sold (2) in violation of state, federal, American Indian tribal, or foreign laws or regulations that are fish- or wildlife-related.[123] Violation of foreign laws with respect to only fish and wildlife (the act does not include foreign plants) can trigger Lacey Act offenses. Under the Lacey Act, a defendant may be prosecuted if they did not violate the law in question, but knowingly, or in the exercise of due care, should know, about the illegal nature of the wildlife or wildlife products.

Wildlife traffickers can also be penalized under the Endangered Species Act of 1973 which makes it unlawful for any person, subject to the jurisdiction of the United States, to import, export, offer, sell in interstate or foreign commerce, or to receive, carry, transport, or ship in interstate or foreign commerce in the course of a commercial activity, any endangered or threatened species. This law also implements CITES into law, and prescribes penalties for violations of CITES. Violations under the Endangered Species Act of 1973 can occur without the defendant knowing which species are listed under this law and without intending to violate the law.[124]

Other laws not directly related to wildlife can be used to prosecute wildlife traffickers. For example, wildlife traffickers can be prosecuted as smugglers under Title 18 of the U.S. Code. Violations such as a concealing contraband (e.g., illegal wildlife) upon import, or knowingly receiving, concealing, buying, or selling contraband, or facilitating these actions, might be prosecuted under the smuggling statutes.[125]

International Assistance and Cooperation

The U.S. government participates in several international venues to enhance the visibility of wildlife crime issues and coordinate with other countries and entities to halt wildlife trafficking. In recent years, the United States has provided funding to three primary international conservation programs that address wildlife trafficking: CITES, the Coalition Against Wildlife Trafficking (CAWT), and the ASEAN Wildlife Law Enforcement Network. U.S. contributions fund efforts to facilitate policy approaches and technical expertise to assist developing countries in building their capacity to combat the illegal wildlife trade.

The United States also participates in several other relevant international venues, including the North American Agreement on Environmental Cooperation, Interpol, World Customs Organization, Group of Eight, and additional U.N. bodies. In addition to these organizations, several additional, regional anti-trafficking organizations exist, in which the United States does not play an active role. These include the South Asia Wildlife Trade Initiative, established in February 2008; the European Union's E.U. Enforcement Action Plan to Combat Illegal Wildlife Trade, established in June 2007; and the Lusaka Agreement Task Force, established in 1994. (See *Appendix B* for descriptions.) On November 30, 2009, the State Department-sponsored Coalition Against Wildlife Trafficking (CAWT) reported that representatives from CITES, the International Police Organization (INTERPOL), the U.N. Office on Drugs and Crime (UNODC), and the World Customs Organization (WCO) met jointly for the first time in Vienna, Austria, to develop an international strategy to prevent and combat the illegal trade in wild animals and plants.[126]

The United States does not participate in international efforts to regulate international wildlife trade to prevent disease transmission or invasive species, as no such international organization currently exists. However, some international organizations, of which the United States is a member, are involved in efforts to track major animal diseases and emerging diseases that can be passed from animals to humans. One such effort launched in 2006, the Global Early Warning System for Major Animal Diseases, involves collaboration between the World Health Organization, the World Organization for Animal Health, and the U.N. Food and Agriculture Organization.[127]

CITES

The CITES Secretariat is the primary multilateral organization that regulates trade in wildlife. The United States is one of 172 parties to CITES, which entered into force in March 1973 and established legal guidelines for the international trade of certain wild animals, plants, and derivatives thereof. These animals, plants, and parts are subject to varying degrees of trade regulation, based on their being listed in the appendices of the Convention. Appendix I lists animals and plants that are threatened with extinction and trade in these species is only authorized in exceptional circumstances. Appendix II lists species not immediately threatened with extinction but may become so if trade is not regulated. Appendix III lists species that are regulated within the jurisdiction of at least one CITES party. Trade in Appendix-listed animals and plants is based on a system of government-issued permits and certificates that must be presented before consignments can leave or enter a country. The 15th meeting of the conference of the Parties to CITES is set for March 2010 in Doha, Qatar. Included on the provisional agenda are the subjects of the illegal trade in ivory and elephant specimens, illegal trade in African and Asian rhinos parts and specimens, and a host of other compliance and law enforcement issues.[128]

Many analysts observe, however, that CITES is limited in its ability to monitor illegal wildlife trade and enforce member states' compliance with the provisions of the treaty.[129] CITES, on its own, does not make illegal wildlife trading a crime or prescribe criminal penalties against violators. Instead, the treaty relies on member states to execute national legislation that enforces CITES commitments and to report to the CITES Secretariat cases of noncompliance. A 2003 U.N. report on wildlife crime and CITES, for example, claims that many member states suffer from an inability to enforce wildlife trade laws, and the penalties associated with the laws are so low that they are unlikely to deter potential wildlife criminals.[130] To address flagrant violators of the treaty, the CITES Secretariat does, on occasion, issue notifications informing member states to suspend trade in CITES-listed species with noncompliant countries. Currently, CITES has active suspension notifications against Djibouti, Guinea-Bissau, Liberia, Mauritania, Nigeria, Rwanda, and Somalia.[131] It remains unclear, however, to what extent these suspensions are carried out by member states.[132]

Coalition Against Wildlife Trafficking

Initiated in 2005, the Coalition Against Wildlife Trafficking (CAWT) is a voluntary partnership among governments and non-governmental entities that seeks to raise the political profile of international wildlife crime. CAWT maintains three goals: (1) improve wildlife law enforcement by expanding training, information sharing, and strengthening regional cooperative networks; (2) reduce consumer demand for illegally traded wildlife by raising awareness of its consequences; and (3) broaden support for combating wildlife trafficking at the highest political levels. As the sole founder of this initiative, the United States is serving as the first two-year chair.

Since its inception, CAWT has been active in holding several international training courses about wildlife law enforcement and related topics and conducting awareness activities. Although some observers welcome this relatively new initiative to help raise the profile of wildlife trafficking issues, others perceive that some countries may be hesitant to commit financially to CAWT. As one expert explained in congressional testimony in 2007, CAWT has suffered from a "slow response from other foreign governments."[133] Currently, there are five other countries, besides the United States, involved in CAWT: Australia, Canada, Chile, India, and the United Kingdom. Furthermore, some observers question whether CAWT has been able to define and differentiate its role among U.S. agencies that have responsibilities to combat illegal wildlife trafficking.

ASEAN Wildlife Enforcement Network

In December 2005, the Association of Southeast Asian Nations (ASEAN)[134] launched the ASEAN Wildlife Law Enforcement Network (ASEAN-WEN) as a regional effort to improve cooperation in combating wildlife crime in Southeast Asia. In the ASEAN statement for its launch, member states noted the "need to strengthen enforcement of CITES and other legislation for wildlife protection" and to "address the serious problem caused by illegal domestic and international trade in wild fauna and flora" given that the "available resources for enforcement are inadequate."[135] Although not a member of ASEAN, the United States provides foreign aid for ASEAN-WEN through USAID's ECO-Asia ASEAN-WEN Support Project. Under this USAID program, the United States is assisting ASEAN-WEN to provide development and capacity building for national wildlife crime task forces, regional cooperation and interaction among task forces, and collaboration with the global law enforcement community.[136]

Other regional efforts to combat the illegal wildlife trade similar to ASEAN-WEN have grown in popularity in recent years, though the United States is not as heavily involved in them at this time. These regional efforts are generally perceived by observers as a positive development, as they bolster regional commitments to solve a criminal activity that is inherently transboundary in nature. Some, however, question whether these new initiatives will be sufficient in curtailing the illegal wildlife trade.

ISSUES FOR CONGRESS

The role of Congress in evaluating U.S. policy to combat wildlife trafficking is broad. This section analyzes some issues Congress may choose to consider, which include (1) funding levels for U.S. wildlife trade inspection and investigation capacity; (2) assessing the role of U.S. foreign aid to combat wildlife trafficking; (3) supplementing legislative provisions to encourage private-sector involvement in controlling wildlife trade; (4) evaluating trade sanction laws relative to foreign countries with weak enforcement of wildlife laws; (5) incorporating wildlife trade provisions into free trade agreements (FTAs); and (6) addressing the domestic and international demand for illegal wildlife through public awareness campaigns and non-governmental organization partnerships.

Funding for Domestic and International Wildlife Trade Inspection and Investigation

Some observers suggest that improving U.S. capacity to prevent illegal wildlife from entering the border and combat transnational wildlife crime syndicates may require Congress to fund and authorize additional inspectors at the border. According to FWS, approximately 75% of declared wildlife shipments are not inspected at the border. There are few inspectors in undesignated ports of entry, where undeclared wildlife shipments are rarely checked.[137] Some have suggested that FWS should increase its inspection of declared and undeclared shipments of wildlife in both designated and undesignated ports of entry in the United States. One possibility would be to increase the number of wildlife inspectors, in proportion to the increase in wildlife shipments entering the United States. In recent years, this has not occurred. Since 2000, the number of wildlife inspectors has increased at an annual average of 3.5%, while the number of shipments has increased at an annual average of approximately 7.8%. (See *Table 4.)* The cost of implementing this proposal, however, would likely involve Congress increasing appropriations for FWS, or increasing user fees for inspecting wildlife at the border.[138]

Others suggest increasing the investigative capacity of FWS to address the illegal wildlife trade controlled by organized crime. From 2000 to 2006, the number of special agents for FWS has increased an average of 0.01% annually, while the investigative caseload has increased an average of 9.7% annually. More special agents might result in a greater number of arrests and prosecutions of wildlife smugglers. Further, more agents may increase the FWS capacity to target specific wildlife smuggling rings or to monitor wildlife smuggling in developing countries where it is thought to be most prevalent. The cost of adding more special agents to the FWS may also involve an increase in appropriations by Congress. Some have argued that this cost might be partially offset by fines paid to the government from more prosecutions of wildlife criminals.

Many observers have highlighted the value of recent international law enforcement initiatives to combat illegal wildlife crime.[139] To this end, some suggest that FWS receive additional authorities from Congress to expand its reach beyond the U.S. border. Proponents argue that such a policy could help FWS, in conjunction with foreign counterparts, target more high-value transnational smuggling syndicates. In testimony to the House Natural Resources Committee in 2008, one analyst indicated that such an expansion if FWS authorities could be modeled on U.S. Drug Enforcement Administration authorities, which permit federal drug law enforcement agents to conduct operations internationally as well as to staff numerous country offices worldwide.[140] Critics of this option, however, argue that wildlife crime is not sufficiently a priority policy issue to warrant the attendant budgetary costs that would be associated with such an expansion of FWS authorities.

Foreign Assistance for Combating Wildlife Trafficking

The majority of endangered species in the world are found in developing countries, where there is need for assistance in protecting species and habitats.[141] Some contend that one opportunity to stem the illegal trade in wildlife is to improve the enforcement capacity of developing countries to control the illegal harvest and export of species. Congress could further this option by appropriating new funds or directing funds in pre-existing conservation programs to train and assist foreign wildlife trade officials in monitoring, detecting, and investigating wildlife trafficking.

FWS and other observers have identified building of wildlife law enforcement infrastructure in source countries as a priority for stemming the illegal trade.[142] Options for achieving this include increasing U.S. efforts to train wildlife inspectors and special agents in developing countries where the illegal wildlife trade is flourishing. The justification of such a proposal is based on three premises: (1) direct training of inspectors and special agents in developing countries will increase their capacity to monitor, investigate, and reduce illegal wildlife trade; (2) interaction between FWS agents and agents in developing countries will improve the coordination and communication among agencies when addressing transnational wildlife crimes; and (3) training programs may give some FWS agents the opportunity to assist their foreign counterparts in foreign countries. Currently, FWS has conducted training programs in Africa, Southeast Asia, Mongolia, and other countries and regions. Training for judges and prosecutors is also being done in foreign countries by DOJ. In collaboration with ASEAN-WEN, U.S. officials are training foreign nationals on methods of prosecuting crimes involving trade in illegally taken wildlife and wildlife parts. This training is conducted in conjunction with the ASEAN-WEN Support Group, FWS and several non-governmental organizations (NGOs).

The benefits associated with this proposal would have to be weighed against the costs of increasing training overseas by FWS. To offset these costs, some contend that Congress could direct funds in some conservation programs toward increasing the law enforcement capacity in countries with high wildlife crime. For example, the Tropical Forest Conservation Act[143] authorizes the use of debt-for-nature swaps to create funds that can given as grants to local organizations to improve the security of nature reserves. Species-specific programs under the Multinational Species Conservation Fund address various components of the illegal wildlife trade and conservation, including law enforcement. Some argue for Congress to appropriate more funds for these programs to address training and monitoring needs. Further, some programs administered by USAID under their Environment and Biodiversity programs address the illegal wildlife trade. For example, in FY2005, USAID supported the training of wildlife law enforcement officials in Cambodia to investigate the illegal wildlife trade..[144]

Private-Sector Cooperation

To prevail against wildlife trafficking, many analysts claim that there is a need for more information on international trafficking routes and a need for that information, if or when collected, to be shared among interested parties. Today, national intelligence on environmental crimes is reportedly not collated and disseminated effectively across countries and law enforcement jurisdictions.[145] As a FWS report explains, combating wildlife trafficking today requires "stepped-up intelligence sharing" and "the pursuit of complex, cooperative investigations that stretch across continents."[146] However, the sharing of intelligence with other countries remains a politically sensitive subject. According to another report, "Actionable information is often withheld in order to avoid embarrassing the countries involved or because of the perceived confidentiality of national enforcement processes."[147]

Intelligence sharing may not necessarily require divulging potentially sensitive political information. Some analysts have suggested introducing heightened industry requirements for tracking commercial wildlife shipments.[148] A broad array of trade-tracking technologies could be applied to wildlife products, including satellite monitoring and the use of barcodes, chemical tracers, and radio-frequency ID tags and transponders. These technologies are already used in tracking a wide variety of products, ranging from narcotics to high-value fashion merchandise. Furthermore, recent scientific findings indicate that ivory products can be traced through DNA analysis with significant accuracy, although this technology is not ready for commercial use.[149] Not all source countries, however, especially in the developing world, have the financial resources to commit to potentially costly tracking technologies. Other questions include whether such tracking technologies are reliable, consistent, or feasible for a market, such as the illegal wildlife market, that includes such a wide variety of products. Indeed, such trade tracking options are unlikely to be applicable for regulating small-scale wildlife shipments.

Another option could involve further expansion of partnerships with the private sector and development of models of corporate social responsibility for "soft" regulatory regimes.[150] Such regimes could involve industry certification schemes for manufacturers of traditional Asian medicine products, Internet-based companies that sell wildlife products, the fashion industry, wild game hunting and tour guide operations, and many other businesses that may involve illegal wildlife. In some cases, as with the labeling of traditional Asian medicines, some pilot programs are underway in other countries, such as the United Kingdom. The non-profit organization, International Fund for Animal Welfare (IFAW), has also sought to promote legislation in California to establish a state-wide labeling program for traditional Asian medicines—and Congress may choose to consider establishing similar, national programs.[151] Potential limitations to this option include the possibility that some wildlife commodities may be so valuable, that profits would trump voluntary commitments. This has been seen in the U.S. illegal caviar trade, where companies fraudulently mislabeled tins of illegal caviar.[152]

Trade Sanctions

Some environment analysts have argued that U.S. trade sanctions can be used as a diplomatic tool to encourage other countries to improve their efforts in combating illegal wildlife trafficking.[153] One such tool, which has been used on a bilateral basis, is the 1971 Pelly Amendment to the Fishermen's Protective Act of 1967.[154] This provision involves a two-step sanctioning process, first requiring the Secretary of Commerce or of the Interior to issue a certification notice to the President when "nationals of a foreign country, directly or indirectly, are engaging in trade or taking which diminishes the effectiveness of any international program for endangered or threatened species."[155] The President, in turn, may choose to direct the Secretary of the Treasury to impose sanctions on imports of any products from the offending country for any duration, provided that the sanction is not prohibited by the World Trade Organization.

A total of 23 countries or territories have been certified a total of 36 times under the Pelly Amendment.[156] The majority of certifications were due to commercial whaling and unsustainable fishing practices. The remaining cases involved other endangered wildlife, including Japan in 1991 for trade in sea turtles; and China and Taiwan in 1993 for trade in rhino horn and tiger bone. On only one occasion—Taiwan for trade in rhino and tiger parts and products—has the President imposed sanctions pursuant to the Pelly Amendment. The sanctions temporarily banned the import of certain fish and wildlife products from Taiwan into the United States. After a few years of improvements in Taiwanese wildlife trade controls, including cooperative law enforcement training between FWS and the Taiwanese authorities, the United States terminated its certification of Taiwan in 1997.[157]

The certification status listing and the threat of American sanctions under the Pelly Amendment, however, remains a source of controversy over its effectiveness and legality. On the one hand, it has been credited for pressuring Japan in the 1990s into addressing its illegal trade in sea turtles.[158] In other cases, however, analysts report that the Pelly certification process has had no, or limited, effect on offending nations.[159] Additionally, some analysts argue that its sporadic use since the early 1990s, including no further use of sanctions since Taiwan in 1994, may be a reflection of its ineffectiveness. Other analysts suggest that the U.S. government may have a political disinclination to impose sanctions against countries for wildlife trafficking. As noted earlier, the CITES Secretariat currently identifies seven countries in non-compliance with CITES provisions, none of which are currently certified or sanctioned for their non-compliance. It also remains unclear how the United States monitors and evaluates foreign country compliance with international programs for endangered or threatened species—and how or when such evaluations trigger the certification process.

There also appears to remain some debate surrounding whether the Pelly Amendment sanction violates World Trade Organization (WTO) and General Agreement on Tariffs and Trade (GATT) guidelines. Although Article XX of

GATT allows for certain environmental trade measures to trump the international free trade regime, GATT and WTO have often ruled against unilateral trade restrictions based on environmental conservation statutes. During the one instance in which the United States applied a Pelly sanction, it was against a country that was not a member of GATT or WTO. As a result, it remains to be seen whether a Pelly Amendment sanction would hold up in a WTO dispute challenge.[160] In the meantime, Congress could move to re-evaluate the effectiveness of the Pelly Amendment as a sanctioning tool and conduct oversight on agencies involved in the certification and sanctioning process.

Free Trade Agreements

The increasing globalization of trade, interconnectedness of markets and supply routes, and emergence of transnational businesses has increased the potential for the illegal trade in wildlife. Indeed, some contend that free trade agreements such as the North American Free Trade Agreement (NAFTA) may facilitate the illegal trade in wildlife because of fewer trade restrictions, generally. For example, some argue that a free trade agreement (FTA) with Singapore increased U.S. imports of illegally obtained timber and wildlife from Singapore and other countries that transport products through Singapore.[161] Others argue that a trade agreement with Peru would have led to an increase in exports of illegally logged timber and wildlife to the United States from Peru. To address these environmental concerns and others, some have proposed that FTAs should include specific provisions that direct countries to implement and enforce CITES, and adhere to existing laws regarding the wildlife trade. Congress is responsible for implementing legislation for FTAs, and might consider FTAs with Columbia, Panama, and South Korea in the 111th Congress.

Some of these concerns were addressed in U.S.-Peru Trade Promotion Agreement (TPA).[162] The TPA requires that Parties adopt laws and measures to fulfill its obligations under multilateral environmental agreements, such as CITES. Further, the TPA would require Parties to enforce their own environmental laws and would establish a policy mechanism to address public complaints that a Party is not effectively enforcing its environmental laws whether or not the failure is trade related. Complaints could be filed by individuals and firms of each Party to the agreement and would be addressed according to a set of procedures outlined in the TPA.[163] An annex on forest sector governance in the TPA specifically addresses the Parties commitment to combat trade associated with illegal logging and illegal trade of wildlife.[164]

The framework for the environmental section in U.S.-Peru TPA could be modified to address the illegal wildlife trade in future agreements with countries that have a significant illegal wildlife trade. Proponents of this view see several benefits to including environmental provisions to deter the illegal wildlife trade in free trade agreements. The FTA may increase the awareness of the illegal wildlife trade and create additional enforcement mechanisms to address trade violations (e.g., dispute mechanisms within the agreement). Further, agreements can provide a layer of assurances that Parties comply with international treaties and enforce their environmental laws. If there is a mechanism for third parties (e.g., outside groups, such as NGOs) to verify compliance and report violations to a committee, supporters assert that it might uncover more wildlife crimes.

A potential drawback of this proposal is that requirements for compliance might require additional funding. If funding is not available, resources might be allocated away from other enforcement and monitoring activities to meet the conditions of the agreement. If the agreement allows outside parties to monitor and conduct investigations into possible violations, some within the country might view this as an infringement on national sovereignty.

Public Awareness and Government-NGO Cooperation

One potential strategy to combat the illegal trade in wildlife is to reduce demand for wildlife. Supporters of this view suggest raising public awareness through public service announcements and campaigns to educate consumers, retailers, and importers of wildlife products. In some cases, as with many tourists, consumers are simply unaware of laws prohibiting the import of products made of protected wildlife. Retail shop-keepers, manufacturers, as well as import-export suppliers may also benefit from learning about the availability of sustainable alternatives and the potential consequences of illegal wildlife trade.

U.S. government and non-governmental organization (NGO) campaigns aimed at demand reduction, domestically and internationally, are ongoing. In October 2007, for example the State Department identified Bo Derek as a "Special Envoy of the Secretary of State for Wildlife Trafficking Issues." Together with Assistant Secretary of State for Oceans, Environment and Science, Claudia McMurray, Derek conducted a series of outreach events to raise public awareness about the illegal global trade in wildlife in Southern Florida, which is one of the major points of entry for legal and illegal wildlife. In Afghanistan, there has been some concern that U.S. personnel may be attempting to bring back to the United States furs and other wildlife artifacts that are protected under CITES, Afghanistan law, and U.S. and miliary laws. To address this the Department of Defense, in concert with officials from the State Department, Environmental Protection Agency, and the non-profit Wildlife Conservation Society, organized information sessions to educate U.S. personnel about illegal wildlife and the consequences of fostering demand for such wildlife products.[165]

Some reports indicate that these public awareness campaigns may show results. The wildlife protection NGO WildAid, for example, launched a reportedly successful series of public advertisements and short films to create awareness about the impacts of the sharkfin trade among consumers in Asia; the campaign reported a 50-70% decrease in demand in some markets.[166] However, it remains to be seen whether future campaigns can show similar results and if these campaigns can effect long-term changes in consumer culture. Congress might play a role in the use and evaluation of demand-side strategies in several ways. For example, Congress could conduct oversight of existing demand-side reduction programs, evaluating the effectiveness of demand-side programs and assessing what policy options may exist to enhance the cost-effectiveness of demand-side anti-trafficking initiatives. Additionally, Congress could direct funds or require U.S. agencies to include demand-side reduction programs in their anti-wildlife trafficking efforts.

APPENDIX A. SELECTED LAWS RELATED TO THE WILDLIFE TRADE

African Elephant Conservation Act[167]

This act establishes as U.S. policy the goals of assisting in conservation and protection of the African elephant. This law directs the Secretary of the Interior to review export controls of raw African elephant ivory in producing states and import controls in raw ivory destination countries. If source or transit countries are found lacking in adequate management of ivory trade, the Secretary of the Interior can issue a moratorium on the import of raw and worked African elephant ivory into the United States. The law also makes illegal the (1) import of raw African elephant ivory from any country other than ivory producing states; (2) the export of raw ivory from the United States; (3) the import of raw or worked ivory from other countries in violation of their laws or of CITES regulations; (4) the import of worked ivory from other countries unless that country certifies that the ivory was derived from legal sources; (5) the import of raw or worked ivory from a country under moratorium; and (6) the sale of raw or worked ivory in the United States from importers or exporters that have not obtained permission to do so by the Secretary of the Interior.

Alien Species Prevention and Enforcement Act of 199 [168]

This act defines what types of plants and animals are "nonmailable," or prohibited from being sent to Hawaii using postal services. Specifically, nonmailable animals include injurious animals prohibited under 18 U.S.C. §42 and illegally taken wildlife prohibited under 16 U.S.C. §3372, are nonmailable.

Animal Health Protection Ac [169]

This act aims to regulate interstate and foreign commerce to prevent, detect, control, and eradicate animal diseases and pests that can affect the livestock industry. Under this act, the Secretary of Agriculture is authorized to prohibit or restrict the import, entry, export, and movement in interstate commerce of any animal, article, or means of conveyance, or use of any means of conveyance or facility if determined to be necessary to prevent the introduction or dissemination within the United States of any pest or disease of livestock.

Animal Welfare Act [170]

This act regulates interstate and foreign trade, traffic, transport, or other commerce of animals to (1) insure that animals intended for use in research facilities, for exhibition purposes, or for use as pets are provided humane care and treatment; and (2) assure the humane treatment of animals during transport in commerce.

Among other stipulations, this law requires that animals in commerce must be marked or identified in a humane manner, and includes standards for handing, housing, feeding, watering, sanitation, ventilation, shelter from extremes of weather and temperature, and other guidelines. Further, this law prohibits buying, selling, delivering, or transporting animals for participation in animal fighting ventures.

Antarctic Conservation Act of 1978 [171]

This act provides for the conservation of wildlife and plants of Antarctica, consistent with the Antarctic Treaty and Protocol. The act makes it unlawful for any U.S. citizen to knowingly receive, acquire, transport, offer for sale, sell, purchase, import, export, or have custody, control, or possession of any native bird, mammal, plant, or invertebrate from Antarctica.

Antarctic Marine Living Resources Convention Act of 1984 [172]

This act makes it unlawful to ship, transport, offer for sale, sell, purchase, import, export, or have custody, control or possession of any Antarctic marine living resource, or part or product thereof, known to have been harvested in violation of U.S. laws consistent with the Convention on the Conservation of Antarctic Marine Living Resources. Antarctic marine living resources include finfish, mollusks, crustaceans, and all other species of living organisms, including birds, found south of the Antarctic convergence.

Bald and Golden Eagle Protection Act [173]

This act prohibits the taking, possession, selling, purchasing, bartering, offering to sell, purchase or barter, transporting, exporting, or importing of any bald or golden eagle, alive or dead, or any part, nest, or egg thereof. Under certain instances, the Secretary of the Interior may permit exceptions to this law. Exceptions include instances that are compatible with the preservation of the bald or golden eagle.

Additionally, specimens may be permitted for scientific or exhibition purposes of public museums, scientific societies, zoos, for religious purposes of Native American tribes, and if necessary for the protection of certain interests in a particular locality.

Dog and Cat Protection Act of 2000[174]

This law prohibits imports, exports, sale, manufacture, offer for sale, transport, and distribution in the United States of dog and cat fur products. The purpose of this law is to ensure that U.S. market demand does not provide an incentive to slaughter dogs or cats for their fur.

Endangered Species Act of 1973[175]

This act establishes a U.S. program for the conservation of endangered and threatened species, consistent with CITES and other international agreements. The law prohibits any person subject to the jurisdiction of the United States to engage in any trade in any specimens contrary to the provisions of CITES, or to possess any specimens traded contrary to the provisions of CITES.

Further, if the Secretaries of the Interior and of Commerce determines a species to be endangered or threatened, this law prohibits any such species from being imported, exported, taken, possessed, sold, delivered, carried, transported, shipped by any means, sold or offered for sale in interstate or foreign commerce. Under certain circumstances, some U.S. persons may be permitted to take or import listed species.

Fisherman's Protective Act of 1967 (Pelly Amendment)[176]

This act establishes provisions to protect U.S. vessels on the high seas and in the territorial waters of foreign countries. Located within this law is the so-called Pelly Amendment,[177] which establishes restrictions on imports of fishery and wildlife products from countries that violate international fishery or endangered or threatened species programs. Specifically, the law directs the Secretary of Commerce and/or of the Interior to certify to the President when nationals of a foreign country directly or indirectly conduct operations in a manner or under circumstances that diminish the effectiveness of conservation programs for fish and endangered or threatened species. Once certified, the President may direct the Secretary of Treasury to prohibit the import of any products from the offending country for any duration, as the President determines is appropriate and to the extent that such prohibitions are sanctioned by the World Trade Organization and other multilateral trade agreements.

Fur Seal Act of 1966[178]

This act prohibits any person to transport, import, offer for sale, or possess at any port or place or on any vessel, subject to the jurisdiction of the United States, fur seals or the parts thereof, including, but not limited to, raw, dressed, or dyed fur seal skins, except under certain circumstances.

Lacey Act[179]

This act seeks to aid in restoring U.S. birds that have become scare or extinct and to regulate the introduction of American or foreign birds or animals in localities where they are not native. All but the first section of the law has since been repealed.

In the original, however, this act prohibited any person or persons to import into the United States any foreign wild animal or bird except under special permit from the U.S. Department of Agriculture.

Lacey Act Amendments of 1981[180]

This act makes it unlawful to import, export, transport, sell, receive, acquire, or purchase any fish or wildlife already taken, possessed, transported, or sold in violation of state, federal, tribal, or foreign wildlife laws or regulations. The Lacey Act also requires that all shipments of wildlife or wildlife products be accurately marked or labeled on shipping containers; it is a violation to transport wildlife and wildlife products under falsely marked containers. The Lacey Act contains provisions that restrict the import or transport of species deemed injurious or potentially injurious to human beings, agriculture, horticulture, forestry, and fish and wildlife resources of the United States. The statute applies only to wild mammals, birds, fish, amphibians, reptiles, mollusks, and crustaceans. It does not apply, for example, to insects, plants, and fungi.[181]

Marine Mammal Protection Act of 1972[182]

This act establishes a moratorium on the taking and import of marine mammals and marine mammal products. It is unlawful to use any port, harbor, or other place under jurisdiction of the United States to take or import marine mammals and marine mammal products. Further, it is unlawful to transport, purchase, sell, export, or offer to purchase, sell, or export such animals taken on the high seas or in waters or land under the jurisdiction of the United States. Some exceptions to this moratorium are allowed, such as the taking of marine mammals and marine mammal products for scientific research and other purposes.

Marine Turtle Conservation Act [183]

This act seeks to assist in conserving marine turtles and in nesting habitats in foreign countries by supporting and providing financial resources for projects to conserve the nesting habitats, and marine turtles in those habitats, and to address other threats to the survival of marine turtles. With regard to the trade in marine turtles, this law states that it will use conservation projects to prevent the illegal trade in marine turtles, among other goals. There are no specific prohibitions on trade of marine turtles in this law.

Migratory Bird Treaty Act[184]

The act was enacted in 1918 to implement the International Convention for the Protection of Migratory Birds signed by the United States and Great Britain (acting for Canada). With exceptions listed in this act, it shall be unlawful "at any time, by any means, or in any manner, to pursue, hunt, take, capture, kill, attempt to do these acts, [or] possess ... any migratory bird, [or] any part, nest, or eggs of any such bird.... " Specifically in relation to trade, it is unlawful to sell or transport migratory birds as defined in the act and associated products contrary to the laws of the State, Territory, or district in which it was captured, killed, or taken. These conditions also apply to the import of birds and associated materials from any Province in Canada. This applies to migratory species native to the United States and its Territories.

Neotropical Migratory Bird Conservation Act[185]

This act provides grants to conserve the hundreds of bird species that migrate between North and South America and the Caribbean. Conservation also includes law enforcement under this act. Further, the act authorizes the Secretary of the Interior to support and coordinate existing efforts to conserve neotropical birds.

Public Health Service Act[186]

This act addresses the importation of wildlife that might be carrying communicable diseases to humans. Specifically, §264(a) authorizes the Surgeon General to enforce regulations that "are necessary to prevent the introduction, transmission, or spread of communicable diseases from foreign countries into the States or possessions.... " The Surgeon General is authorized to inspect, fumigate, disinfect, sanitize, and destroy animals or articles found to be infected or contaminated "as to be sources of dangerous infection to human beings.[187]"

Rhinoceros and Tiger Conservation Act of 1994[188]

This act seeks to assist in the conservation of all species of rhinos and tigers, including those already listed as protected species from trade under CITES and U.S. regulations. The law specifically prohibits the sale, import, and export of products intended for human consumption or application that contain or are labeled or advertised as containing, any substance derived from any species of rhino or tiger.

Wild Bird Conservation Act of 1992[189]

This act limits or prohibits imports of exotic birds when necessary to ensure that wild exotic bird populations are not harmed by removal of exotic birds from the wild for trade and that exotic birds in trade are not subject to inhumane treatment. The law includes provisions to limit or prohibit U.S.

imports of exotic bird species covered by CITES and authorizes moratoria on the import of species not necessarily covered by CITES.

APPENDIX B. ADDITIONAL INTERNATIONAL EFFORTS TO COMBAT WILDLIFE CRIME

North American Agreement on Environmental Cooperation

In conjunction with the North American Free Trade Agreement (NAFTA), Canada, Mexico, and the United States also signed the North American Agreement on Environmental Cooperation and created the Commission for Environmental Cooperation in 1993. This international organization was established to address regional environmental concerns, help prevent potential trade and environmental conflicts, and promote the effective enforcement of environmental law, including those protecting wildlife. Through its North American Working Group on Environmental Enforcement and Compliance Cooperation, this organization provides senior wildlife enforcement officials from NAFTA countries a forum for regional cooperation, expertise exchange, and enforcement capacity building. One component of this working group is the North American Wildlife Enforcement Group (NAWEG), created in 1995.

Interpol

As parts of its efforts to address environmental crimes, Interpol established a Working Group on Wildlife Crime in 1994. The wildlife working group's primary goals are to coordinate information sharing related to wildlife crime on an international scale and to facilitate and coordinate operational enforcement activity. To achieve this, Interpol maintains an international network for the exchange of information, enhances domestic operations in member countries through cooperation and coordination activities, and assists in training wildlife enforcement officers in developing countries. In 1996, a full-time officer was appointed to manage Interpol's wildlife crime programs.

World Customs Organization

With its specialty in international trade and customs administration and 171-country membership, including the United States, the World Customs Organization works with other international organizations and member countries on wildlife trafficking and other issues. Since July 1996, the World

Customs Organization and the CITES Secretariat have maintained a legal framework for international cooperation to exchange information related to wildlife crime and promote awareness and training for customs and management authorities at the national level.

Group of Eight

During the March 2007 Group of Eight (G-8) meeting of environmental ministers in Postdam, Germany, the attendees committed to the "Postdam Initiative—Biological Diversity 2010."[190] This agreement aims to strengthen international efforts to combat the illegal trade in wildlife, among other concerns, by 2010.

UN Commission on Crime Prevention and Criminal Justice

Acknowledging that the trafficking of forest products, including wildlife, is often linked to organized crime and can involve the same actors who traffic drugs, arms, and persons, the United States, in conjunction with Indonesia, Australia, the Philippines, and Thailand, sponsored a resolution that urges countries to fight forest and wildlife crime by strengthening law enforcement cooperation, combating criminal groups operating within their borders, and cooperating through the U.N. Convention Against Transnational Organized Crime and the U.N. Convention Against Corruption. The resolution, first presented for adoption in 2006, was adopted on April 25 at the 2007 commission meeting in Vienna.[191]

Lusaka Agreement and Task Force

The Lusaka Agreement on Co-operative Enforcement Operations Directed at Illegal Trade in Wild Fauna and Flora is a formal intergovernmental organization, which entered into force in 1996, under the auspices of the U.N. Environment Programme. The group aims to improve wildlife crime law enforcement cooperation and capacity-building.

As part of the Lusaka Agreement, the member states launched the Lusaka Task Force as a permanent law enforcement institution to facilitate international cooperation in carrying out wildlife crime investigations in Africa.

The Task Force, which includes as parties to the agreement the governments of the Republic of Congo, Kenya, Lesotho, Uganda, Tanzania, and Zambia, is sometimes referred to as the "African Interpol for Wildlife."

Enforcement Action Plan to Combat Illegal Wildlife Trade

Unveiled in 2007, the E.U. Enforcement Action Plan to Combat Illegal Wildlife Trade seeks to improve wildlife trade enforcement across the E.U. as well as in wildlife source countries. In the source countries, the E.U. aims to provide law enforcement capacity building as well as increase awareness of illegal wildlife trade.

South Asia Wildlife Trade Initiative

Established in February 2008 under the South Asia Cooperative Environmental Programme, the South Asia Wildlife Trade Initiative includes country representatives from Afghanistan, Bangladesh, Bhutan, India, the Maldives, Nepal, Pakistan, and Sri Lanka. During the initiative's first regional workshop from January 31 to February 1, 2008, senior wildlife officials from these countries agreed to increased cooperation in regulating their wildlife trade. The country representatives established two efforts to realize this goal: the South Asia Experts Group on Wildlife Trade and the South Asia Regional Strategic Plan on Wildlife for 2008 through 2013.

End Notes

[1] 16 U.S.C. §701, as amended.

[2] Lacey Act Amendments of 1981 (P.L. 97-79, as amended); Endangered Species Act of 1973 (P.L. 93-205, as amended).

[3] Congress implemented CITES under the Endangered Species Act of 1973. P.L. 96-159 designates the Secretary of the Interior, acting through the U.S. Fish and Wildlife Service (FWS), as both the CITES Management and Scientific Authority. See CRS Report RL32751, The Convention on International Trade in Endangered Species of Wild Fauna and Flora (CITES): Background and Issues, by Pervaze A. Sheikh and M. Lynne Corn.

[4] Attempts to quantify the value of illegal wildlife trade have resulted in many estimates that vary in size and scope. For a range of estimates on the size of the illegal wildlife trade see U.S. Interagency Working Group, International Crime Threat Assessment Report (December 2000); U.S. Department of State, Bureau of Oceans and International Environment and Scientific Affairs, "Announcing the Formation of the Coalition Against Wildlife Trafficking," September 22, 2005; United Kingdom National Wildlife Crime Unit, "Wildlife Crime," at http://www.nwcu.police.uk/ pages/wildlifecrime/crime.asp; and Interpol, "Wildlife Crime," at http://www.interpol.int/Public/EnvironmentalCrime/ Wildlife/Default.asp.

[5] U.S. Agency for International Development (USAID), "ASEAN Wildlife Enforcement Network," undated brochure, at http://usaid.eco-asia.org/files/fact_sheets/ASEAN_ WEN. pdf.

[6] U.S. Department of State, Bureau of Oceans and International Environmental and Scientific Affairs, "Fact Sheet: Against Wildlife Trafficking – Working Together to End the Illegal Trade in Wildlife," January 30, 2009.

[7] CITES covers approximately 5,000 species of animals and 28,000 species of plants.

[8] Duncan Brack, "Combating International Environmental Crime," Global Environmental Change, vol. 12, no. 2 (July 2002), pp. 143-147.

[9] Jolene Lin, "Tackling Southeast Asia's Illegal Wildlife Trade," Singapore Year Book of International Law and Contributors, vol. 9 (2005), pp. 191-208.

[10] Richard T. Corlett, "The Impact of Hunting on the Mammalian Fauna of Tropical Asian Forests," Biotropica, vol. 39, no. 3 (2007), pp. 292-303.

[11] Maylynn Engler and Rob Perry-Jones, Opportunity or Threat: The Role of the European Union in the Global Wildlife Trade (Brussels, Belgium: TRAFFIC Europe, 2007).

[12] Randi Alacron, "The Convention on the International Trade of Endangered Species: The Difficulty in Enforcing CITES and the United States Solution to Hindering the Trade in Endangered Species," N.Y. International Law Review, vol. 14, no. 2 (2001), pp. 105-108.

[13] U.S. Department of the Interior, Fish and Wildlife Service (FWS), Office of Law Enforcement, Annual Reports, FY2000-FY2006, at http://www.fws.gov/le/AboutLE /annual.htm; and personal communication with FWS officials, February 20, 2008. Figures are in constant FY2008 U.S. dollars.

[14] Ibid.

[15] This analysis is based on the types and quantities of wildlife shipments refused entry at the U.S. border. Although the data may reflect the categories of illegal wildlife in demand by consumers, the data may not accurately reflect the full magnitude of the illegal trade in the United States. See U.S. Department of the Interior, FWS, Office of Law Enforcement, Intelligence Unit, U.S. Illegal Wildlife Trade: LEMIS Data Analysis and Risk Assessment, November 2005.

[16] U.S. Department of the Interior, FWS, Office of Law Enforcement, Strategic Plan, 2006-2010, at http://www.fws.gov/le/AboutLE/OLEStrategicPlanDec2005.pdf.

[17] Richard Ellis, Tiger Bone and Rhino Horn: The Destruction of Wildlife for Traditional Chinese Medicine (Washington, DC: Island Press, 2005).

[18] Dee Cook, Martin Roberts, and Jason Lowther, The International Wildlife Trade and Organised Crime: A Review of the Evidence and the Role of the UK (United Kingdom: World Wildlife Fund, 2002), p. 18.

[19] FWS, U.S. Illegal Wildlife Trade: LEMIS Data Analysis and Risk Assessment.

[20] Gavin Hayman and Duncan Brack, "International Environmental Crime: The Nature and Control of Environmental Black Markets," The Royal Institute of International Affairs (2002), p. 114. See also Cook, Roberts, and Lowther, The International Wildlife Trade and Organised Crime, p. 10.

[21] See, for example, Emily Wax, "Poaching and Population Threatens India's Tigers," Washington Post, October 16, 2007; "Trade in Wildlife: Just Let Them Get on with It," The Economist, May 29, 2008.

[22] Hayman and Brack, "International Environmental Crime," p. 144.

[23] Report of the U.N. Secretary-General, "Progress Made in the Implementation of Economic and Social Council Resolution 2001/12 on Illicit Trafficking in Protected Species of Wild Flora and Fauna," U.N. Economic and Social Council, Commission on Crime Prevention and Criminal Justice, 11th session, Vienna, Austria, February 26, 2002, p. 6; Report of the U.N. Secretary-General, "Illicit Trafficking in Protected Species of Wild Flora and Fauna and

Illicit Access to Genetic Resources," U.N. Economic and Social Council, Commission on Crime Prevention and Criminal Justice, 12th session, Vienna, Austria, March 4, 2003, p. 9.

[24] See, for example, Greg Warchol, Linda Zupan, and Willie Clack, "Transnational Criminality: An Analysis of the Illegal Wildlife Market in Southern Africa," International Criminal Justice Review, vol. 13, no. 1 (2003), p. 7; Lin, "Tackling Southeast Asia's Illegal Wildlife Trade," p. 198; and Hayman and Brack, "International Environmental Crime."

[25] Warchol, Zupan, and Clack, ibid, p. 24; Hayman and Brack, "International Environmental Crime," p. 7.

[26] See, for example, Warchol, Zupan, and Clack, ibid.

[27] Report of the U.N. Secretary-General (2003), p. 10; and U.S. Interagency Working Group, International Crime Threat Assessment.

[28] FWS, Office of Law Enforcement, Strategic Plan, 2006-2010, p. 7.

[29] Cook, Roberts, and Lowther, The International Wildlife Trade and Organised Crime, pp. 19-20; Report of the U.N. Secretary-General (2002), pp. 5-6.

[30] International Fund for Animal Welfare (IFAW), "Caught in the Web: Wildlife Trade on the Internet," 2005, at http://www.ifaw.org/ifaw/dfiles/file_562.pdf.

[31] International Union for Conservation of Nature and Natural Resources (IUCN), African Elephant Status Report 2007: An Update from the African Elephant Database, Occasional Paper Series of the IUCN Species Survival Commission, no. 33 (2007). According to the IUCN, primary reasons for the elephant population's decline include habitat loss and fragmentation, human-elephant conflict, and poaching for elephant meat and ivory. International trade in Asian elephant ivory is also illegal under CITES.

[32] Under CITES, ivory from southern African elephants from Botswana, Namibia, Zimbabwe, and South Africa is allowed to be traded. Most recently, in 2007, CITES approved a second auction of 60 tons of government-stockpiled elephant ivory from Botswana, Namibia, and South Africa; CITES has yet to decide when this second auction will take place and to which countries it will be sold.

[33] "CITES Permits 60 Tons of Elephant Ivory to Be Sold," Environmental News Service, June 4, 2007.

[34] T. Miliken, R.W. Burn, and L. Sangalakula, "The Elephant Trade Information System (ETIS) and the Illicit Trade in Ivory," report produced by TRAFFIC in advance of the 15th Conference of the Parties of CITES, CoP15 Doc. 44.1 Annex, October 14, 2009.

[35] The price of ivory may vary significantly, depending on its size, quality, and type. Additionally, experts highlight distinctions between forest elephant tusks and savannah elephant tusks; the forest elephant tusk is known to be more desirable for its pinkish hue and density, which makes it preferable for carving. See, for example, Esmond Martin and Daniel Stiles, "U.S. Exposed as Leading Ivory Market," Report prepared for Care for the Wild International, June 5, 2007.

[36] TRAFFIC, "Monitoring of Illegal Trade in Ivory and Other Elephant Specimens," Fourteenth Meeting of the Conference of the Parties, June 3, 2007, at http://www.cites.org/eng/cop/14/doc/E14-53-2.pdf. The study reports that the number of "big seizures," defined as seizures involving more than 1 metric ton of ivory, grew from 17, between 1989 through 1997, to 32, between 1998 through 2006. In 2002, Singapore officials confiscated a single shipment of more than 6 tons of illicit ivory—the largest seizure since the 1989 ban.

[37] According to IUCN, the distribution of African elephants vary across western, central, southern, and eastern Africa. Southern Africa accounts for approximately 39% of the total species' known population, Central Africa accounts for 29%, East Africa accounts for 26%, and West Africa accounts for 5%. The accuracy of the population estimates also varies

across the continent, with estimates in conflict zones or countries emerging from conflict being especially limited. See Nigel Hunter, Esmond Martin, and Tom Milliken, "Determining The Number of Elephants Required to Supply Current Unregulated Ivory Markets in Africa and Asia," Pachyderm, no. 36 (January-June 2004), pp. 116-128; and IUCN, African Elephant Status Report 2007.

[38] TRAFFIC, "Monitoring of Illegal Trade in Ivory and Other Elephant Specimens." Thailand is also a heavily-implicated elephant ivory trading country, but some of its ivory trade includes Asian elephant ivory as well.

[39] See, for example, "Sudan is 'Centre of Ivory Trade,'" BBC News, March 14, 2005; and Esmond Martin, "Large Quantities of Illegal Ivory for Sale in Sudan," Report for Care for the Wild International, March 14, 2005. Some 75% of the ivory is reportedly bought by Chinese customers, many of whom are working in Sudan in the oil industry.

[40] Martin, "Large Quantities of Illegal Ivory for Sale in Sudan"; and "Illegal Ivory Seized in Taiwan," World Wildlife Fund, July 7, 2006; also based on CRS discussions with Interpol law enforcement officials familiar with the case in 2007.

[41] Samuel Wasser et al., "Using DNA to Track the Origin of the Largest Ivory Seizure Since the 1989 Trade Ban," Proceedings of the National Academy of Science of the United States of America vol. 104, no. 10 (March 6, 2007), at http://depts.washington.edu/conserv/web-content/Press/Wasser%20et%20al%202007.pdf.

[42] U.S. Fish and Wildlife Service (FWS), "Ivory Traffickers Nabbed in International Sting Operation," November 18, 2009; and FWS, Office of Law Enforcement, "Case at a Glance: U.S.-Royal Thai Police Ivory Investigation," at http://www.fws.gov/home/feature/2010/pdf/12510USThaiIvorySB.pdf.

[43] One possible explanation might be that as a species becomes depleted and rare, the costs of finding and harvesting individuals becomes prohibitive; species are likely to become extinct economically before they become extinct biologically.

[44] Steven Broad et al., The Nature and Extent of Legal and Illegal Trade in Wildlife.

[45] See Evan Bowen-Jones and Stephanie Pendry, "The Threats to Primates and Other Mammals from the Bushmeat Trade in Africa and How This Could Be Diminished," Oryx, vol. 33, no. 3 (1999), pp. 233-247.

[46] Ellis, Tiger Bone and Rhino Horn.

[47] Martin Schlaepfer et al., "Challenges in Evaluating the Impact of the Trade in Amphibians and Reptiles on Wild Populations," BioScience, vol. 55, no. 3 (2005), pp. 256-264.

[48] In some tropical forests in Africa and Asia, for example, the loss of some mammals may slow vegetation recovery because of the dependence on mammals as seed dispersers and pollenators. See Richard T. Corlett, "Frugivory and Seed Dispersal in Degraded Tropical East Asian Landscapes," in D.J. Levey et al., eds., Seed Dispersal and Frugivory: Ecology, Evolution, and Conservation (Wallingford, UK: CABI Publishing, 2002), pp. 451-465.

[49] For more on harmful non-native species, see CRS Report RL30123, Invasive Non-Native Species: Background and Issues for Congress, by M. Lynne Corn et al.

[50] One study estimates the annual economic damage of non-native species in the United States to be approximately $123 billion. See David Pimentel, Lori Lach, Rodolfo Zuniga, and Doug Morrison, "Environmental and Economic Costs of Nonindigenous Species in the United States," BioScience, vol. 50 (January 2000), pp. 53-65.

[51] Of 212 non-native vertebrate species that established wild populations in the United States, 48 species (23%) were originally imported as cage birds or other pets. U.S. Congress, Office of Technology and Assessment, Harmful Non-Indigenous Species in the United States, OTA-F-565 (Washington: GPO, 1993).

[52] See discussion on the Lacey Act and the injurious species provisions in Appendix A .

[53] David Wilcove et al., "Quantifying Threats to Imperiled Species in the United States," BioScience, vol. 48 (1998), pp. 607-615.

[54] Burmese pythons are illegal in some states (e.g., Illinois). In other states, it is illegal to release them into the wild (e.g., Florida, where over 1,000 are estimated to be in the wild). See Florida Fish and Wildlife Conservation Commission, Notice of New Florida Rules and Regulations Concerning Possession of Captive Wildlife, at http://myfwc.com/permits/Docs/ SynopsisCaptiveWLRuleChanges.pdf.

[55] Defenders of Wildlife, "Broken Screens: The Regulations of Live Animal Imports into the United States," 2007, at http://www.defenders.org/resources/publications/ programs_ and_policy/international_conservation/broken_screens/ broken_screens_report.pdf.

[56] FWS, Office of Law Enforcement, Strategic Plan, 2006-2010.

[57] U.S. Congress, Senate Committee on Environment and Public Works, Importation of Exotic Species and their Impact on Public Health and Safety, hearing, 108th Cong., 1st sess., July 17, 2003, at http://epw.senate.gov/ hearing_statements.cfm?id=212889.

[58] William B. Karesh, "Wildlife Trade and Global Disease Emergence," Emerging Infectious Diseases, vol. 11, no. 7 (2005), pp. 1000-1002.

[59] William B. Karesh et al., "Implications of Wildlife Trade on the Movement of Avian Influenza and other Infectious Diseases," Journal of Wildlife Diseases, vol. 43, no. 3 (2007), pp. 55-59.

[60] Peter Daszak, "Risky Behavior in the Ebola Zone," Animal Conservation, vol. 9 (2006), pp. 366-367.

[61] U.S. General Accounting Office, "West Nile Virus Outbreak, Lessons for Public Health Preparedness," September 2000, GAO/HEHS-00-180, p. 68.

[62] Some examples include a psittacosis infection in custom officers in Belgium after being exposed to illegally imported parakeets, and an avian influenza virus carried by crested hawk eagles smuggled into Europe. Bruno B. Chomel, "Wildlife, Exotic Pets, and Emerging Zoonoses," Emerging Infectious Diseases, vol. 13, no. 1 (2007), pp. 6- 11.

[63] Y. Guan et al., "Isolation and Characterization of Viruses Related to the SARS Coronavirus from Animals in Southern China," Science, vol. 302, no. 5643 (2003), pp. 276-278.

[64] Center for Food Security and Public Health, Iowa State University, Heartwater, at http://www.cfsph.iastate.edu/ Factsheets/pdfs/heartwater.pdf.

[65] See CRS Report RL33795, Avian Influenza in Poultry and Wild Birds, by Jim Monke and M. Lynne Corn.

[66] In response to the outbreak, CDC banned the import of all African rodents into the United States and prohibited the transportation, sale, distribution or release of prairie dogs and African rodents that might have been carrying the disease. For more information on monkeypox, see CRS Report RS21557, Monkeypox: Technical Background and Outbreak Implications for Bioterrorism Preparedness, by Dana A. Shea, Frank Gottron, and Holly Harvey.

[67] Center for Non-Proliferation Studies, Monterey Institute of International Studies, "Chemical and Biological Weapons Resource Page," at http://cns.miis.edu/research/cbw/possess.htm.

[68] Ibid.

[69] See CRS Report RS21557, Monkeypox: Technical Background and Outbreak Implications for Bioterrorism Preparedness, by Dana A. Shea, Frank Gottron, and Holly Harvey.

70 This bill has been referred to the Committee on Natural Resources.

71 Testimony of Gail Golab, Director of Animal Welfare Division, American Veterinary Medical Association, House Natural Resources Committee, Subcommittee on Fisheries, Wildlife,

and Oceans, Legislative Hearing on H.R. 2964 and H.R. 5534, hearing, 110th Cong., 2nd sess., March, 11, 2008.

[72] Testimony of Sian Evans, Director of the DuMond Conservancy for Primates and Tropical Forests, House Natural Resources Committee, Subcommittee on Fisheries, Wildlife, and Oceans, Legislative Hearing on H.R. 2964 and H.R. 5534, hearing, 110th Cong., 2nd sess., March, 11, 2008.

[73] See Elizabeth L. Bennett et al., "Hunting for Consensus: Reconciling Bushmeat Harvest, Conservation, and Development Policy in West and Central Africa," Conservation Biology, vol. 21, no. 3 (2006), pp. 884-887.

[74] Bushmeat Crisis Taskforce, Global Human Health Fact Sheet, October 2003.

[75] Ibid.

[76] Evan Bowen-Jones, "Bushmeat: Traditional Regulation or Adaptation to Market Forces," in Oldfield, ed., The Trade in Wildlife.

[77] Zinta Zommers and David Macdonald, Wildlife Trade and Global Disease Emergence, Office of Science and Innovation, Trade and Industry Division, 2006.

[78] Emmanuel De Merode and Guy Cowlishaw, "Species Protection, the Changing Informal Economy, and the Politics of Access to the Bushmeat Trade in the Democratic Republic of Congo," Conservation Biology, vol. 20, no. 4 (2006), pp. 1262-1271.

[79] Testimony of Marshall Jones, Deputy Director, FWS, in Senate Committee on Environment and Public Works, Importation of Exotic Species and Their Impact on Public Health and Safety.

[80] Declared bushmeat shipments might be checked by FWS at the border, but there is no requirements for quarantine to check bushmeat for disease. FWS inspectors are not trained in disease detection. However, the USDA's Animal and Plant Health Inspection Service (APHIS) may confiscate illegal bushmeat detected at the border, if suspected of carrying disease that might affect livestock. If the bushmeat is suspected carrying a disease harmful to humans, CDC is contacted.

[81] Gao Feng et al., "Origin of HIV-1 in the Chimpanzee Pan Troglodytes Troglodytes," Nature, vol. 397 (1999), pp. 436-441.

[82] Karesh, "Wildlife Trade and Global Disease Emergence," pp. 1000-1002.

[83] Centers for Disease Control and Prevention, visited at http://www.cdc.gov /ncidod/ monkeypox/animals.htm, February 23, 2008.

[84] See, for example, Mara Zimmerman, "The Black Market for Wildlife: Combating Transnational Organized Crime in the Illegal Wildlife Trade," Vanderbilt Journal of Transnational Law, vol. 36 (2003), pp. 1672-1673; and Greg Warchol, "The Transnational Illegal Wildlife Trade," Criminal Justice Studies, vol. 17, no. 1 (March 2004), p. 58.

[85] Report of the U.N. Secretary-General (2002), p. 6; Report of the U.N. Secretary-General (2003), pp. 9-12. See also Jonathan Kazmar, "The International Illegal Plant and Wildlife Trade: Biological Suicide," U.C. Davis Journal of International Law and Policy, vol. 6, no. 105 (Winter 2000).

[86] Report of the U.N. Secretary-General (2003), p. 9.

[87] Report of the U.N. Secretary-General (2002), p. 6; Report of the U.N. Secretary-General (2003) p. 11; Kazmar, "The International Illegal Plant and Wildlife Trade"; and Cook, Roberts, and Lowther, The International Wildlife Trade and Organised Crime, p. 15.

[88] Report of the U.N. Secretary-General (2002), p. 6; and Report of the U.N. Secretary-General (2003), p. 11.

[89] FWS, Office of Law Enforcement, Strategic Plan, 2006-2010, p. 7.

[90] Report of the U.N. Secretary-General (2002), p. 6; Kazmar, "The International Illegal Plant and Wildlife Trade"; and Report of the U.N. Secretary-General (2003), p. 12.

[91] Testimony of Steven R. Galster, House Natural Resources Committee, "Poaching American Security," Hearing, March 5, 2008.

[92] Cook, Roberts, and Lowther, The International Wildlife Trade and Organised Crime, p. 23.

[93] Report of the U.N. Secretary-General (2002), pp. 6-7.

[94] "First National Report on the Traffic of Wild Animals," RENCTAS, 2001, p. 53.

[95] Report of the U.N. Secretary-General (2002), pp. 6-7.

[96] "Organized Criminal Gangs Deal Wildlife and Drugs," Environment News Service, June 18, 2002.

[97] Based on discussions with several Interpol law enforcement officials in 2007.

[98] Mark Schoofs, "Traffic Jam: As Meth Trade Goes Global, South Africa Becomes a Hub—Cape Town Gangs Barter Rare Shellfish for Drugs; Chinese, Russian Ties," Wall Street Journal, May 21, 2007.

[99] Report of the U.N. Secretary-General (2002), p. 6.

[100] Notably, the map is not indicative of zones where terrorist activity is necessarily occurring and where organized wildlife smugglers are necessarily operating.

[101] See Louise I. Shelly and John T. Picarelli, "Methods Not Motives: Implications of the Convergence of International Organized Crime and Terrorism," Policy Practice and Research, vol. 3, no. 4 (2002).

[102] See Rohan Gunaratna, Inside Al Qaeda: Global Network of Terror (New York: Columbia University Press, 2002).

[103] Lin, "Tackling Southeast Asia's Illegal Wildlife Trade."

[104] Somali warlords are generally not considered international terrorists. Interpol officials, however, say wildlife poaching is linked to at least one known Somali warlord, allegedly known to have protected Al Qaeda operatives allegedly involved in the 1998 Kenya and Tanzania U.S. Embassy bombings and the 2002 Kenya hotel bombing. For a description of terrorism activity linked to Somalis, see U.S. Department of State, Office of the Coordinator for Counterterrorism, Country Report on Terrorism, April 30, 2007. Some Interpol officials speculate that the poached wildlife could be used to finance Somali warlord activities, or possibly even Al Qaeda terrorism activities; CRS has yet to find public evidence to support these speculations. There remains some debate among analysts, however, regarding the level of sufficient evidence linking Somali warlords to the terrorist suspects involved in the bombings described above. For more of this debate, see CRS Report RL33911, Somalia: Current Conditions and Prospects for a Lasting Peace, by Ted Dagne.

[105] "Poaching for Bin Laden," The Guardian, May 5, 2007; Sharon Begley, "Extinction Trade," Newsweek, March 1, 2008. HUJI-B and JMB are designated as Foreign Terrorist Organizations by the U.S. Department of State.

[106] See, for example, R. Thomas Naylor, "The Underworld of Ivory," Crime, Law, and Social Change, vol. 42, no. 4-5 (January 2005), p. 261.

[107] Chris R. Shepherd and Vincent Nijman, "The Trade in Bear Parts from Myanmar: An Illustration of the Ineffectiveness of Enforcement of International Wildlife Trade Regulations," Biodiversity Conservation, vol. 17, no. 1 (January 2008), p. 35.

[108] "Southeast Asia's Illegal Wildlife Trade," National Public Radio, November 3-5, 2003, at http://www.npr.org/ programs/re/archivesdate/2003/nov/wildlife/index.html.

[109] Naylor, "The Underworld of Ivory," pp. 261-277; Warchol, "The Transnational Illegal Wildlife Trade," p. 58; Warchol, Zupan, and Clack, "Transnational Criminality: An Analysis of the Illegal Wildlife Market in Southern Africa," p. 5; and John Nielsen,

"Confronting Central Africa's Poaching Crisis," National Public Radio, January 12, 2003, at http://www.npr.org/templates/story/story.php?storyId=912962.

[110] See also "DNA Test Pinpoints Elephant Poaching, Aiding Conservation: Genetic Evidence Could Prove Key in Halting the Illegal Slaughter of Africa's Elephants for their Ivory Tusks," Scientific American, February 26, 2007; and "War and Politics Threaten Congo's Endangered Rhinos," The New York Times, March 28, 2005.

[111] In addition to ivory, RENAMO reportedly ran rackets in rhino horn, rare hardwoods, stolen gemstones, and counterfeit currency. See Naylor, "The Underworld of Ivory," p. 278.

[112] Most of the posted wildlife inspectors are located at the Los Angeles, New York, New Jersey, and Miami ports of entry. FWS, U.S. Illegal Wildlife Trade: LEMIS Data Analysis and Risk Assessment.

[113] FWS, Importing and Exporting Your Commercial Wildlife Shipment, at http://www.fws.gov/le/ImpExp/ CommWildlifeImportExport.htm.

[114] Interview with Tom Tidwell, Senior Special Agent, FWS, November 2007.

[115] P.L. 100-478, as amended.

[116] Under the Homeland Security Act of 2002 (P.L. 107-296), some of APHIS' border security responsibilities were transferred to the Department of Homeland Security. These duties include border inspection of shipments and baggage containing plant, animal, and agricultural products that could harbor pests and diseases. APHIS retains the responsibility to create inspection policies and train inspection agents. The specific functions that were transferred from APHIS to DHS are included in an agreement at http://www.aphis.usda.gov/plant_health/moa_dhs/index.shtml.

[117] See U.S. Department of Agriculture, APHIS, "Smuggling Intervention and Trade Compliance Program," at http://is.aphis.usda.gov/lpa/pubs/pub_smuggling.html.

[118] 16 U.S.C. §§1801-1882, as amended; P.L. 94-265, as amended.

[119] CDC has the authority to prevent the spread of communicable diseases under the Public Health Service Act (42 U.S.C. §201 et seq.).

[120] For full list of quarantinable diseases, see Executive Order 13295, "Revised List of Quarantinable Communicable Diseases,"April 4, 2003; and "Executive Order: Amendment to E.O. 13295 Relating to Certain Influenza Viruses and Quarantinable Communicable Diseases," April 1, 2005.

[121] As of 2004, ENRD employed more than 400 attorneys to handle more than 10,000 cases per year in all federal jurisdictions. Approximately 30 ENRD attorneys specialize in prosecuting environmental crime cases. See Jim Rubin and Shata Stucky, "Fighting Black Markets and Oily Water: The Department of Justice's National Initiatives to Combat Transnational Environmental Crime," Sustainable Development Law and Policy, vol. 4 (2004), pp. 21-26.

[122] Because illegal wildlife traffickers are often caught before violating the Lacey Act, conspiracy is a way to charge the wrongdoers for committing a crime. The crime of conspiracy occurs when "two or more persons conspire" to violate the Lacey Act. The conspiracy offense can act as further arsenal against wildlife violators. In fact, charging an individual with conspiracy may be considered a graver offense than the contemplated crime and can lead to harsher penalties.

[123] Some address the categories labeled above for violating the Lacey Act as the two steps necessary for prosecution. See Testimony of Eileen Sobeck, Deputy Assistant Attorney General, Environment and Natural Resources Division, U.S. Department of Justice, in U.S. Congress, House Natural Resources Committee, Subcommittee on Fisheries, Wildlife, and Oceans, Illegally Harvested Plants, hearing, 110th Cong., 1st sess., October 16, 2007.

[124] John T. Webb and Robert S. Anderson, "Prosecuting Wildlife Traffickers: Important Cases, Many Tools, Good Results," United States Attorneys' Bulletin (December 1999), pp. 4-10.

[125] For example, see 18 U.S.C. §545.

[126] Coalition Against Wildlife Trafficking (CAWT), "New Strategy to Combat Global Wildlife Crime," November 30, 2009.

[127] World Health Organization, "Launch of Global Early Warning System for Animal Diseases Transmissible to Humans," Press Release, at http://www.who.int/mediacentre/news/new/2006/nw02/en/index.html.

[128] Available at http://www.cites.org/eng/cop/15/doc/index.shtml.

[129] Hayman and Brack, "International Environmental Crime," p. 22.

[130] Report of the U.N. Secretary-General (2003).

[131] CITES Notification to the Parties, No. 2003/027 (May 6, 2003); No. 2004/055 (July 30, 2004); No. 2005/038 (July 19, 2005); No. 2006/073 (December 14, 2006); No. 2006/074 (December 14, 2006).

[132] Rosalind Reeve, "Wildlife Trade, Sanctions, and Compliance: Lessons from the CITES Regime," International Affairs, vol. 82, no. 5 (2006), pp. 881-897; and Zimmerman, "The Black Market for Wildlife," p. 1666.

[133] Testimony Crawford Allan, World Wildlife Fund, in U.S. Congress, House Natural Resources Committee, Subcommittee on Fisheries, Wildlife, and Oceans, Endangered Species Treaty Meeting, hearing, 109th Cong., 2nd sess., May 3, 2007.

[134] The ten members of ASEAN are Burma, Brunei, Cambodia, Indonesia, Laos, Malaysia, the Philippines, Singapore, Thailand, and Vietnam.

[135] "ASEAN Statement on Launching of the ASEAN Wildlife Law Enforcement Network at the Special Meeting of the ASEAN Ministers Responsible for the Implementation of CITES," Bangkok, Thailand, December 1, 2005.

[136] USAID, "Environmental Cooperation-Asia (ECO-Asia) ASEAN Wildlife Enforcement Network."

[137] CBP checks a percentage of all shipments and contacts FWS if wildlife shipments are intercepted.

[138] FWS finalized a rule to gradually increase inspection fees and update license and fee requirements for importing and exporting wildlife in December 2008. Fees have not been increased since 1996. Raising fees is intended to recover some costs of inspecting shipments.

[139] See for example, testimony by Claudia A. McMurray, House Natural Resources Committee, "Poaching American Security: Impact of Illegal Wildlife Trade," March 5, 2008.

[140] Testimony of Steven R. Galster, House Natural Resources Committee, "Poaching American Security: Impact of Illegal Wildlife Trade," March 5, 2008.

[141] Alacron, "The Convention on the International Trade of Endangered Species."

[142] FWS, Office of Law Enforcement, Strategic Plan, 2006-2010, p. 5.

[143] 22 U.S.C. §2431

[144] USAID, USAID Biodiversity and Forestry Conservation Programs, FY2005, 2007, at http://www.usaid.gov/our_work/environment/biodiversity/pubs/biodiversity_conservation_forestry_2005_508_ready_102507.pdf.

[145] Hayman and Brack, "International Environmental Crime," p. 24; FWS, Office of Law Enforcement, Strategic Plan, 2006-2010, p. 5.

[146] FWS, Office of Law Enforcement, Strategic Plan, 2006-2010, p. 5.

[147] Hayman and Brack, "International Environmental Crime," p. 24.

[148] Ibid., pp. 26-27.

[149] Samuel Wasser et al., "Using DNA to Track the Origin of the Largest Ivory Seizure Since the 1989 Trade Ban."

[150] Hayman and Brack, "International Environmental Crime," p. 32.

[151] International Fund for Animal Welfare (IFAW), "Traditional Medicine: A Major Threat That Few Suspect," at http://www.ifaw.org/ifaw/general/default.aspx?oid=180459.

[152] Andrew C. Revkin, "Vast Caviar Smuggling Case Brings Guilty Pleas," The New York Times, July 22, 2000.

[153] Theodora Greanias, "A Tool of Persuasion: International Wildlife Conservation," Endangered Species Bulletin (July 1998); and Andrew F. Upton, "The Big Green Stick: Reducing International Environmental Degradation through U.S. Trade Sanctions," Boston College Environmental Affairs Law Review, vol. 22 (1994-1995), pp. 671-692.

[154] 22 U.S.C. §1978, as amended.

[155] Additionally, this law requires the Secretaries to issue a certification notice to the President when foreign countries are allowing fishing operations to occur that diminish the effectiveness of an international fishery conservation program

[156] These countries include (dates of certification in parentheses): Japan (1974, 1988, 1991, 1992, 1995, 2000); the former Soviet Union (1974, 1985); Chile (1978); Peru (1978); South Korea (1978); Norway (1986, 1990, 1992, 1993); Taiwan (1989, 1991, 1993); Mexico (1991); Colombia (1992); Canada (1992, 1996); Malaysia (1992); Netherlands Antilles (1992); Singapore (1992); Spain (1992); United Kingdom (1992); Venezuela (1993); Vanuatu (1992); Costa Rica (1992); France (1992); Italy (1992); Panama (1992, 1993); China (1993); and Iceland (2004).

[157] "Termination of the Pelly Amendment Certification of Taiwan," Federal Register, vol. 62, no. 83 (April 30, 1997); and Greanias, "A Tool of Persuasion."

[158] Peter H. Sand, "Whither CITES? The Evolution of a Treaty Regime in the Borderland of Trade and Environment," European Journal of International Law, vol. 8 (1997), p. 39.

[159] See, for example, Steve Charnovitz, "Environmental Trade Sanctions and the GATT: An Analysis of the Pelly Amendment on Foreign Environmental Practices," American University Journal of International Law and Policy, vol. 9 (1993-1994), pp. 751-807.

[160] For a discussion of this, see Scott C. Owen, "Might a Future Tuna Embargo Withstand a WTO Challenge in Light of the Recent Shrimp-Turtle Ruling?," Houston Journal of International Law (Fall 2000).

[161] Environmental Investigation Agency, "America's Free Trade for Illegal Timber," 2006.

[162] United States-Peru Trade Promotion Agreement, Chapter 18, Environment, at http://www.ustr.gov/Trade_Agreements/Bilateral/Peru_TPA/Final_Texts/Section_Index.html.

[163] Ibid.

[164] This annex requires Peru to: (1) increase the number and effectiveness of personnel to enforce laws; (2) provide criminal and civil liability at adequate deterrent levels for actions that undermine the sustainable management of forests and violate laws pertaining to the harvest and trade of timber; (3) verify that timber products are harvested in compliance with all laws; and (4) monitor the timber trade within the country, among other things.

[165] "Environmental Education for Afghans Essential, U.S. Officials Say," Armed Forces Press Service, August 15, 2007.

[166] Hayman and Brack, "International Environmental Crime," p. 31.

[167] 16 U.S.C. §§4201 et seq.; P.L. 100-478, as amended. Congress also enacted another elephant conservation law, the Asian Elephant Conservation Act of 1997 (16 U.S.C. §§4261-4266;

P.L. 105-96, as amended). This law, however, does not include any provisions that restrict the trade in Asian elephant ivory.

[168] 39 U.S.C. §3015 note; P.L. 102-393.

[169] 7 U.S.C. §8301 et seq.; P.L. 107-171.

[170] 7 U.S.C. §§2131 et seq.; P.L. 89-544, as amended.

[171] 16 U.S.C. §§2401 et seq.; P.L. 95-541, as amended.

[172] 16 U.S.C. §§2431 et seq.; P.L. 98-623.

[173] 16 U.S.C. §§668 et seq.; P.L. 86-70, as amended.

[174] 19 U.S.C. §1308; P.L. 106-476.

[175] 16 U.S.C. §§1531-1544; P.L. 93-205, as amended.

[176] 22 U.S.C. §§1971 et seq.; P.L. 90-482, as amended.

[177] 22 U.S.C. §1978; P.L. 92-219, as amended.

[178] 16 U.S.C. §§1151 et seq.; P.L. 89-702, as amended.

[179] 16 U.S.C. §701; 31 Stat. 187, as amended.

[180] 16 U.S.C. §§3371 et seq.; P.L. 97-79, as amended.

[181] There are currently 26 individual species, genera, or families listed as injurious species.

[182] 16 U.S.C. §§1361 et seq.; P.L. 92-522, as amended.

[183] 16 U.S.C. §§6601 et seq.; P.L. 108-266.

[184] 16 U.S.C. §§703 et seq.; 40 Stat. 755, as amended.

[185] 16 U.S.C. §§6101 et seq.; P.L. 106-247, as amended.

[186] 42 U.S.C. §264(a); 58 Stat. 703, as amended.

[187] A list of embargos on specific species can be found at http://www.cdc. gov/ncidod/dq/animal.htm.

[188] 16 U.S.C. §§5301 et seq.; P.L. 103-391, as amended.

[189] 16 U.S.C. §§4901 et seq.; P.L. 102-440.

[190] Countries represented at the meeting included the United States, Germany, France, Italy, Japan, Russia, and the United Kingdom.

[191] U.N. Commission on Crime Prevention and Criminal Justice, "International Cooperation in Preventing and Combating Illicit International Trafficking in Forest Products, Including Timber, Wildlife and Other Forest Biological Resources," Australia, Indonesia, Philippines, Thailand and United States of America: revised draft resolution, April 25, 2007.

In: Illicit Trade in Wildlife and the Economics ... ISBN: 978-1-62417-877-1
Editor: Rolande Gagnier

Chapter 2

THE ECONOMICS OF AGRICULTURAL AND WILDLIFE SMUGGLING*

Peyton Ferrier

ABSTRACT

The United States bans imports of certain agricultural and wildlife goods that can carry pathogens or diseases or whose harvest can threaten wildlife stocks or endanger species. Despite these bans, contraband is regularly uncovered in inspections of cargo containers and in domestic markets.

This study characterizes the economic factors affecting agricultural and wildlife smuggling by drawing on inspection and interdiction data from USDA and the U.S. Fish and Wildlife Service and existing economic literature.

Findings reveal that agricultural and wildlife smuggling primarily include luxury goods, ethnic foods, and specialty goods, such as traditional medicines. Incidents of detected smuggling are disproportionately higher for agricultural goods originating in China and for wildlife goods originating in Mexico.

Fragmentary data show that approximately 1 percent of all commercial wildlife shipments to the United States and 0.40 percent of all U.S. wildlife imports by value are refused entry and suspected of being smuggled.

---

* This is an edited, reformatted and augmented version of a United States Department of Agriculture publication, Economic Research Report Number 81, dated September 2009.

Keywords: Smuggling, illicit trade, SPS, quarantine, endangered species, CITES

LIST OF ACRONYMS

AMS	Agricultural Marketing Service (USDA)
APHIS	Animal and Plant Health Inspection Service (USDA)
AQAS	Agricultural Quarantine Activities System
AQIM	Agricultural Quarantine Inspection Monitoring
CBP	Customs and Border Protection (DHS)
CITES	Convention for the Trade of Endangered Species
DHS	U.S. Department of Homeland Security
EAN	Emergency Action Notice
ESA	Endangered Species Act
FDA	Food and Drug Administration (U.S. Department of Health and Human Services)
FWS	U.S. Fish and Wildlife Service (U.S. Department of the Interior)
GAO	Government Accountability Office
LEMIS	Law Enforcement Management Information System
OTA	Office of Technology Assessment
PPQ	Plant Protection and Quarantine
SITC	Smuggling Interdiction and Trade Compliance group (of APHIS)
SPS	Sanitary and Phytosanitary
USDA	U.S. Department of Agriculture
WADS	Work Activities Data System
WTO	World Trade Organization

SUMMARY

The United States bans imports of certain agricultural and wildlife goods that may pose unique risks to the environment or the agricultural economy. Despite these bans, contraband is regularly discovered during inspections of cargo containers and found for sale in domestic markets. Very little is known about the size and scope of such smuggling.

WHAT IS THE ISSUE?

Banned agricultural goods can carry diseases, pathogens, foreign organisms, or contaminants that threaten the health of humans, animals, and plants; the environment; and the trade status of U.S. exports. Trade in banned wildlife goods may also endanger the survival of a species. Yet, banned goods still appear in U.S. markets. This study examines agricultural and wildlife smuggling—its specific characteristics, including estimations of its size and scope; its responsiveness to economic incentives; and regulations and efforts to reduce its risks.

WHAT DID THE STUDY FIND?

Agricultural and wildlife smuggling primarily involves luxury items and jewelry made from animal parts; ethnic foods, such as szechuan peppers and tropical fruits; and specialty goods, including traditional medicines. These types of items are also likely to command high prices relative to their cost and size. Small amounts of smuggled goods occasionally move over pedestrian and personal vehicle pathways, but commercial volumes of smuggled goods are likely to be transported through international shipping channels.

Among all countries exporting to the United States, incidents of detected smuggling are more prevalent with goods shipped from Mexico (wildlife) and China (agricultural). However, both countries are major trade partners with the United States, and U.S. imports from both have increased dramatically over the last 25 years. Interdictions of meat products are particularly high from China. Inspections data reveal that Mexico has the highest amount of refused shipments of fruits and vegetables, though it is also the leading exporter of these products to the United States. Mexico and Russia have the highest rates of refusal of wildlife goods. Refused goods from Mexico typically include live animals, of which birds are a particular concern due to their potential for spreading diseases and pathogens. Differences in smuggling prevalence rates across countries are attributed to differences in the types of goods affected by trade prohibitions, the visibility of smuggled goods, and the targeting of enforcement resources.

Based on fragmentary inspections data, wildlife smuggling accounts for approximately 1 percent of commercial wildlife shipments to the United States and 0.4 percent of the total value of U.S. wildlife imports. Fragmentary interdiction data show that agricultural smuggling is small, accounting for 0.03 percent of total agricultural imports from China, the country with the highest reported proportions and volumes of smuggled imports. Still, these figures, along with most widely reported estimates, are inexact due to the potential for bias in the data.

Smuggling is motivated by profits. Criminal penalties and fines represent a cost of smuggling, while the difference between the price of a smuggled good at its origin and at its (prohibited) destination represents its return. Governments may reduce the incentive to smuggle both by increasing the cost through higher penalties and tighter enforcement and by reducing its return. To reduce price disparities that encourage smuggling, governments may compensate producers affected by trade bans and eradication programs, ensure that close-substitute goods can gain legal trade access, and reduce the size of markets impacted by a trade ban through regionalization. A small but growing literature finds empirical support that smuggling responds to incentives related to enforcement, detection, and profitability.

How Was the Study Conducted?

The analysis is supported by data on random and targeted inspections of agricultural cargo from USDA's Animal and Plant Health Inspection Service, interdiction data from the U.S. Fish and Wildlife Service, and trade data from the U.S. Census Bureau.

Introduction

Between 1998 and 2007, the real values of U.S. agricultural and wildlife imports increased 70 percent (Census Bureau) and 108 percent (FWS, 2008), respectively. Agricultural and wildlife imports, however, can introduce invasive species or disease-carrying pathogens and thus pose unique risks to the domestic environment and the agricultural economy. Furthermore, trade in certain wildlife goods places pressure on natural stocks abroad and can endanger the survival of animal and plant species, including elephants, exotic birds, and whales.

To mitigate these risks, regulators rely on trade restrictions allowed under the World Trade Organization's (WTO) Agreement on the Application of

Sanitary and Phytosanitary Measures (SPS Agreement) and the Convention for the Trade of Endangered Species (CITES). In many cases, specific commodities are restricted based on country of origin, destination within an importing country, and time of year (for seasonal pests). Enforcement of these restrictions is multifaceted. Infrastructure and logistical constraints make the complete physical inspection of all imported shipments impractical. Instead, inspection occurs at different rates (the percentage of shipments actually inspected) and intensities (the proportion of goods in a shipment actually physically observed). Even the most thorough enforcement process may fail to prevent all restricted goods from entering commercial trade.

Smuggling, defined as the illegal import of contraband goods, is an ancient activity. However, only with the emergence of modern pathology and the progressive, environmental, and conservation movements since the late 19th century have trade restrictions been widely adopted for goods harming public health, agricultural productivity, and the environment. These trade restrictions and regulations may disproportionately harm some consumers by constraining consumption choices or artificially benefit some domestic producers if used to mask protectionist measures. International treaties and agreements constrain the extent to which the United States may ban agricultural imports without repercussion from trade partners. They also require that the United States ban certain wildlife goods. Smuggling circumvents those bans and, despite significant resources devoted to enforcement, banned and contaminated goods still appear in U.S. markets. Integrated global markets, lower transportation costs, and rising incomes have not only increased the levels of both total trade and imports but also allowed for the more rapid movement of exotic pathogens and plant pests across borders and ecosystems and increased the size of potential markets for limited wildlife resources.

The costs of agricultural and wildlife smuggling are difficult to quantify in specific terms. Interpol estimates that the value of the illegal global wildlife trade alone ranges between $7 billion and $20 billion annually and cites it as the second largest form of illegal trade (Interpol, 2006; 2008).[1]

No comparable estimate of the size of agricultural smuggling is available, but its consequences are acknowledged to be significant due to the large potential risk posed by very small amounts of biological material that may enter a country with the smuggled goods. For example, an outbreak of Exotic Newcastle Disease among poultry in California in 2003 is thought to have spread from smuggled game birds from Mexico. As a result, California poultry farmers incurred eradication costs of approximately $168 million. A 2005 shipment of 450 citrus cuttings carrying citrus canker was intercepted by U.S.

Customs and Border Protection (CBP); if the disease had become established in the United States, potential costs to the U.S. citrus industry have been estimated at between $173 million and $890 million. For invasive species, the Office of Technology Assessment estimates the annual costs at $4.9 billion (OTA, 1993). During the 1990s, spending on emergency eradication programs for invasive species in the United States increased from $10.4 million to $232 million (Lynch and Lichtenberg, 2006). Moreover, the risks of wildlife and agricultural smuggling are interrelated as wild plants and animals are more likely to carry agriculturally significant pathogens than farm-raised animals or to become invasive themselves.[2]

Based on an analysis of data on shipment inspection and interdiction, this study examines the smuggling of agricultural and wildlife goods into the United States—including its specific characteristics and its responsiveness to economic factors.

THE ECONOMICS OF AGRICULTURAL AND WILDLIFE SMUGGLING

According to Naim (2005, p. 239), illicit trade is driven by high profits and not low morals. At its core, smuggling is a market phenomenon, and trade bans, by their very nature, encourage smuggling. Taxes, tariffs, and trade restrictions create gaps between the price that sellers receive and the price that buyers pay, the difference of which is the return to smuggling. Illicit trade is self-reinforcing because reductions in smuggling increase its profitability. The lost trade from this market disequilibrium represents that maximum amount of goods that might be smuggled in the absence of enforcement or legal penalty (Ferrier, 2008).

A Model of Smuggling

The market incentive for smuggling is the disparity between the price of a good at its origin and destination. Price disparities have been shown to encourage smuggling in the work of Fisman and Wei (2004) for tariff evasion generally; Thursby et al. (1991), Saba et al. (1995), and Goel (2004) for cigarettes; and Golub and Mbaye (2007) for sugar, wheat, and rice. A weak rule of law can lower the probability of penalty or apprehension and encourage smuggling as shown by Ivanova (2007) for ozone-depleting substances and Fisman and Wei (2004) for artwork.

Von Hippel and Von Hippel (2002) show that the presence of substitutes, which may reduce demand and make it more elastic, also reduces smuggling in the case of wildlife goods. Yang (2008) shows that methods of smuggling to evade tariffs in the Philippines adjust when changes are made to inspection-targeting regimes.

In Ferrier's (2008) model of the illicit agricultural and wildlife trades, demand for smuggled goods is developed from trade theory while the supply of smuggled goods is developed from the economic model of crime first posed by Becker (1968). Several importers and exporters engage in competitive free trade (with several countries of *origin* exporting to one *destination*) and the price of traded goods differs only by transit costs.

A trade ban for a single country of origin restricts that country's exports so that its markets would transact under autarky if no smuggling occurred. Figure 1 depicts a market where two origin markets export to a single destination. Under free trade, prices net of transit costs across the three markets are equal and the sum of exports from origins one and two is equal to total imports to the destination. When a trade ban blocks imports from origin one to the destination market, prices rise in both the destination and the (unrestricted) origin two from P_1^{FT} and P_3^{FT} to P_1^{TB} and P_3^{TB} simultaneously raising origin two's exports and lowering the destination's total imports, until an equilibrium is reached where these two values are equal. Simultaneously, prices fall in origin one from P_2^{FT} to P_2^{TB}.,where no exports occur. With the ban in place, a wedge emerges between the price at which a good is sold in origin one and the price at which a good is purchased in the destination market (net of transit costs). This price wedge represents the return to successful smuggling.

The magnitude of the price wedge will influence its prevalence, and its size depends critically on several observable market factors, including market size, the magnitude of trade flow, the number of trade partners, and, most importantly, the relative elasticities of supply and demand. Generally, more inelastic supply and demand in the restricted origin leads to a larger price decrease, while more inelastic supply and demand in the remaining free trade areas leads to larger price increases. The price effects are not symmetric, however.

A small number of trade partners in the free-trade area with elastic supply and demand can sufficiently adjust production to replace the lost supply of imports and mitigate price swings.

In the restricted origin, the lack of alternative outlets for excess supply results in large extended price decreases. Goods likely to have inelastic demand include ethnic foods (certain spices, ethnic specialty goods), luxury food items (caviar), and medicinal items. As discussed later, the data show that these goods are all intercepted regularly.

The supply of smuggled goods depends on the willingness of risk-averse agents faced with an uncertain payoff to supply criminal trading services. Given the level of fines and the probability of apprehension, some level of fine makes traders indifferent in choosing to earn the lower price at the restricted origin or the higher price at the destination with the probability of incurring a fine and forfeiture of goods. In general, as the price wedge between the restricted origin and the destination increases, traders will smuggle goods in larger quantities.

As more goods are smuggled, the price disparity falls. An equilibrium occurs when the increased amount of smuggling lowers the price disparity to make traders indifferent to smuggling additional goods abroad or selling in the legal, but lower priced, domestic market. Compensation to producers affected by trade bans and eradication programs, encouragement of the development of acceptable close substitute goods, and reductions in the size of markets impacted by trade bans through regionalization can reduce the price disparity that encourages smuggling.

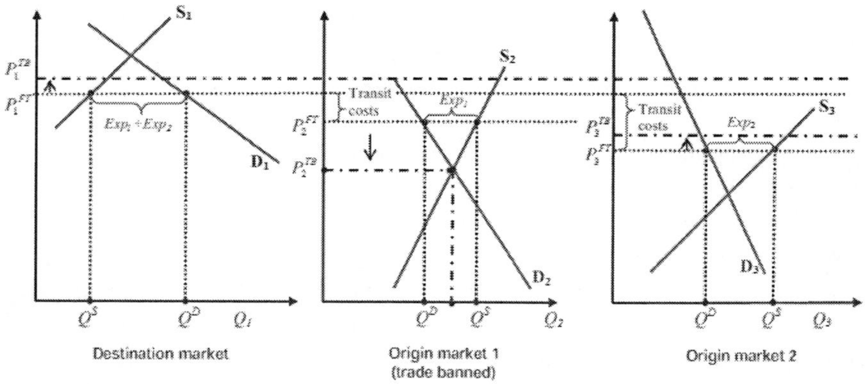

Source: USDA, Economic Research Service.

Figure 1. The free trade and trade ban equilibrium.

Economic Literature on Smuggling

More generally, economists have typically considered several interrelated questions with regard to smuggling. First, what are the costs of smuggling and is smuggling ever beneficial to society? Given the historical orientation of countries toward protectionist trade restrictions, economists (Bhagwati and Hensen, 1973; Kemp, 1976; Norton, 1988; and Martin and Panagariya, 1984) have typically approached smuggling without consideration for externalities, —situations in which a market transaction imparts a cost or benefit to another individual in a way not reflected in market prices. On this score, smuggling is typically found to improve aggregate societal welfare as it moves the market closer to its efficient equilibrium occurring under free trade.

However, when restricted goods impart risks to security, public health, or the environment, smuggled goods create externalities. For example, smuggled goods can potentially introduce foreign plant diseases or pests that reduce agricultural productivity or require expensive eradication measures. These costs may be difficult to quantify, depending on the risk of the contraband goods entering the country, the amount entering, and the uncertain costs that will result if a pest becomes established. For wildlife goods, smuggling can endanger the survival of a species, entailing a loss of biodiversity and aesthetic beauty that is not easily quantified.[3] Because agricultural and wildlife smuggling involves external costs, it differs substantially from ordinary tariff-avoiding smuggling, in which the harm is measured as the lost revenue from the proportion of goods smuggled. The harm of agricultural and wildlife smuggling, alternatively, may increase exponentially with the proportion of goods smuggled if foreign pests are more likely to become established with larger exposure or if threatened species are more likely to become extinct as a result of increased poaching. Moreover, an increased volume of imports would require a falling proportion of goods smuggled simply to maintain the status quo level of exposure to smuggling's associated risks. Concern and regulation surrounding agricultural and wildlife smuggling may arise from human health effects, where the presence of smuggled goods lowers demand for legal goods (if, for example, smuggled goods present a health risk),[4] and stigma effects, where the underlying demand for an illegally traded good may fall due to social pressure.[5]

Other questions considered by economists include the following: how much smuggling occurs and how much does smuggling respond to market forces? Undoubtedly, trade restrictions foster smuggling. Little is known about the illicit agricultural and wildlife trade specifically, relative to other types of illicit trade. Significant differences in the patterns of illegal trade may emerge for two reasons. First, most agricultural and some wildlife goods are likely to be sold in ordinary commercial outlets operating otherwise legally rather than in concealed clandestine outlets (illegal markets).[6] Second, most agricultural and some wildlife goods have both legal and illegal sources. Identifying the relative proportion of legal and illegal trade is challenging due to the possible endogenous nature of enforcement. If contraband is sold in small quantities in legal markets, personnel in interdiction and inspection may be unaware of its occurrence. Alternatively, if contraband is sold openly and is commonly available, inspection and enforcement efforts may be limited in their effectiveness because complete enforcement is difficult.

Regulation

With regard to the risks posed by imports of agricultural and wildlife goods, the government performs three basic functions—*regulation,* to establish the conditions for legitimate imports, including treatments and product requirements; *inspection*, to ensure that those imports satisfy regulations; and *interdiction*, to recover illegally imported material and enforce subsequent penalties. Over time, separate Federal Government agencies emerged to address the regulation, inspection, and interdiction of U.S. imports for different types of risk (see box, “The Evolving Regulatory Structure”). After 2003, agricultural inspection operations (for invasive species) were moved to the newly formed U.S. Department of Homeland Security, while regulatory and interdiction authority of agricultural goods remained with USDA’s Animal and Plant Health Inspection Service (APHIS). All three functions— regulation, inspection, and interdiction—of wildlife goods remained with the U.S. Fish and Wildlife Service (FWS).

Domestically, the Plant Protection Act of 2000 and the Animal Health Protection Act of 2002 delegate to APHIS the authority to promulgate SPS-based trade restrictions. The laws also designate APHIS as the scientific authority in cases where the restrictions are challenged by U.S. trade partners. For example, disputes may arise over the degree to which an invasive species is already established in a country. If a country already has an established pest that is actively controlled, the importing country may not ban trade based on that pest threat. Similarly, APHIS provides evidence to trade partners to defend U.S. exporters against unfounded claims that U.S. goods may carry a disease or pathogen. Internationally, the 1995 Agreement on the Application of Sanitary and Phytosanitary Measures governs disputes over claims that SPS restrictions violate free trade commitments under the General Agreement of Trade and Tariffs.[7] This agreement requires that trade restrictions designed to mitigate SPS risks follow two broad principles—that they not be used to disguise protectionism, and that the restrictions not be arbitrary or discriminatory. Evidence of harm and scientific risk assessment must be provided by an importing country to justify a restriction if challenged. If fumigation or cold treatment by an exporting country mitigates a pest risk or if certain exporting regions within a country can be determined to be pest free, then programs are to be put in place that address the remaining risk without halting all trade.

The harm from the importation of banned wildlife goods (that is, species loss or endangerment) is more diffuse, but certainly falls more squarely on the exporting country as species loss can result in less revenue from ongoing trade and tourism and the loss of a country's ecological distinctiveness. International treaties, therefore, are oriented toward enforcing restrictions on imports determined collectively by member countries. The primary U.S. law regulating wildlife imports is the Endangered Species Act (ESA), which is also the enabling legislation for U.S. participation in CITES.[8] CITES, however, also explicitly allows member states the discretion to enact "stricter domestic measures." As a result, imports of certain species restricted by ESA are not restricted by CITES.[9] Countries enacting discretionary restrictions of wildlife goods have occasionally been accused of being protectionist (Hutton, 2000).

The Evolving Regulatory Structure

Prior to 2003, USDA's Animal and Plant Health Inspection Service (APHIS) performed regulatory, inspection, and interdiction functions for U.S. agricultural imports. After 2003, the agency's inspection responsibilities were consolidated into the newly formed U.S. Department of Homeland Security (DHS). APHIS retained its regulatory responsibilities for assessing pest risk, setting import protocols, and prohibiting certain goods from entering the country.

Following the 2001 terrorist attacks in the United States, information sharing across inspections functions was seen as essential for a comprehensive approach to addressing immediate risk. Customs and Border Protection, under DHS, would inspect imports posing immediate threats, while other existing agencies would inspect goods posing other, but not necessarily immediate, risks.

For this reason, the Fish and Wildlife Service of the U.S. Department of the Interior retained both its regulatory and inspection responsibilities for most wildlife, except for some live plants and fish. Similarly, the Food and Drug Administration of the U.S. Department of Health and Human Services both regulates and inspects agricultural products for pathogens and adulterants by testing and approving pharmaceutical drugs, pesticides, and food production methods for their safety and effectiveness and by sampling cargo containers for proscribed material and contaminants. However, the Customs Service (previously under the U.S. Department of Treasury), which inspects imports for tariff assessment, property rights violations, illegal weapons and narcotics, and other restricted trade, was also moved to Customs and Border Protection under DHS.

CITES has three appendices that proscribe wildlife trade to different extents. Species listed in CITES appendix I are banned from trade entirely. Countries can transfer these species across borders only if the destination is a verified scientific institution or if the species was raised in captivity. Species listed in CITES appendix II can be traded only if the exporting country issues a certificate of origin and obtains a permit certifying that the product's harvest was not detrimental to the country's wild stock. Species listed in CITES appendix III can be traded only if all participating CITES members issue a certificate of origin to document that their exports are not from the country where the wildlife is threatened. The listing country must issue a permit certifying nondetrimental harvest. An exporting country may unilaterally add a species to CITES appendix III. Among all countries, CITES requirements are typically more important but also more burdensome for poor countries that have larger undeveloped regions and greater stocks of highly valuable but endangered wildlife. Relative to developed countries, these poorer countries have more limited infrastructure to enforce harvest regulation, higher returns to illicit exports, and fewer alternative industries for employment.

Methods of Smuggling

Small amounts of smuggled goods occasionally move over pedestrian and personal vehicle pathways, but commercial volumes of smuggled goods are likely to be transported through international shipping channels. To this end, cargo manifests can be falsified so that the product or country of origin is misrepresented or goods can be trans-shipped through countries that do not prohibit imports of the goods (APHIS, 2006). For example, Mexico allows grape imports from Chile as long as the grapes are free of fruit flies, but the United States requires imports of the same Chilean grapes to be fumigated with methyl bromide.

However, U.S. imports of Mexican grapes can enter without treatment (Meissner et al., 2003, pg. 122). Trans-shipping of grapes would involve moving Chilean grapes through Mexico into the United States to misrepresent them as being of Mexican origin and avoid additional fumigation expenses. Similarly, nursery stock from China must remain in Canada for a year before it can be exported to the United States as a Canadian product. Trans-shipping would involve moving the foreign nursery stock into the United States via another country as a way to sidestep the waiting period. Hansen (2000, pp. 175-80) documents how collectors and researchers of rare orchids use trans-shipping to bypass CITES-based import restrictions.

More commonly, though, importers smuggle goods by incorrectly identifying contraband on cargo manifests. Prohibited agricultural goods may be relabeled as permitted goods, or endangered wildlife goods may be labeled as a nonthreatened species.

For example, in 2004, APHIS found a prohibited shipment of frozen chicken feet from China that was labeled as frozen fish. CITES appendix I lists the entire orchid family and the parrot family, with the exception of three varieties, to help prevent the endangered family members from being "mismanifested" as similar looking but nonthreatened species (Roe et al., 2002, p. 27; Hansen 2000). Mismanifesting exploits the difficulties of physically inspecting cargo containers that are large and require space to unpack, especially if the cargo is refrigerated and labeled in a foreign language.

Whether goods are smuggled into the United States for commercial or personal purposes is directly relevant to the enforcement of trade regulations. Travelers smuggling goods for personal purposes may not readily recognize the extent of the trade prohibitions or the potential fines. Commercial importers, on the other hand, must submit manifests detailing the contents of shipping containers, interact more regularly with trade channels, and generally have obvious incentives to become knowledgeable with regulations. Criminal violations under the Endangered Species Act, the Plant Protection Act, and the Animal Health Protection Act may be punishable by fines ranging from $1,000 to $50,000 per occurrence, a year in prison, and the loss of the cargo.

Estimating the Size of Smuggling with Inspections Data

Smugglers seek to avoid discovery, which severely complicates any estimation of the size of smuggling and its responsiveness to regulatory policy. In theory, smuggling is revealed by inspection if three conditions are met. First, all cargo must enter the country through known, legal channels; second, all cargo must be inspected; and third, inspections must reveal perfectly whether imports are illegal. Because smuggled agricultural goods earn only modest markups and are difficult to transport, only a small portion are likely to arrive in noncargo conveyances that circumvent inspection points. This may not be the case for some wildlife goods (e.g., exotic parrots), which earn large returns. Agricultural smuggling is likely to go undetected owing to weaknesses in inspections involving the second and third conditions. Regulatory agencies can inspect all cargo entering the United States comprehensively, but it is prohibitively costly to do so. Comprehensive inspection may require several hours to unpack cargo containers (which may be refrigerated) and overwhelm the capacity of inspectors to process cargo (CBP, 2007b). Thus, some unregulated cargo is not inspected.[10] Moreover, even inspected cargo may contain unrevealed smuggled goods. The intent to smuggle goods may be unclear when goods are imported as when the documentation of a wildlife good's origin or an agricultural good's phytosanitary certificate is missing. More significantly, inspections occur with different levels of intensity. Less rigorous inspections may not always detect smuggling, especially when oriented toward detecting pest infestations rather than smuggling, and may involve only sampling or a visual inspection.

Despite these shortcomings in the inspection process and the potential for biases, this study's estimation of the size of smuggling is based in large part on data gathered in the inspection process depicted in figure 2 (see box, "Alternative Methods for Estimating the Size of Smuggling"). As shown in the figure, producers ship goods to a foreign port of disembarkation. Entry of these goods into the United States may require certification of a particular production process. For example, meats shipped from countries that have experienced outbreaks of BSE require a certificate of origin and a health or inspection certificate; wildlife sales may require similar certificates of origin and nondetrimental harvest. On average, international agricultural shipments require 46 separate documents (AMS, 2004, p. 16).

For U.S. imports, regulated cargo must be inspected for pest risk in the United States or abroad before being released. Goods found with pests are treated, destroyed, or re-exported to another country. When inspectors find a prohibited good or a good containing a pest, they issue an Emergency Action Notice (EAN) to legally document the pest and mitigating actions as well as inform other ports of the potential risk. Goods released for sale in the United States are then entered into customs data, and importers pay applicable duties.

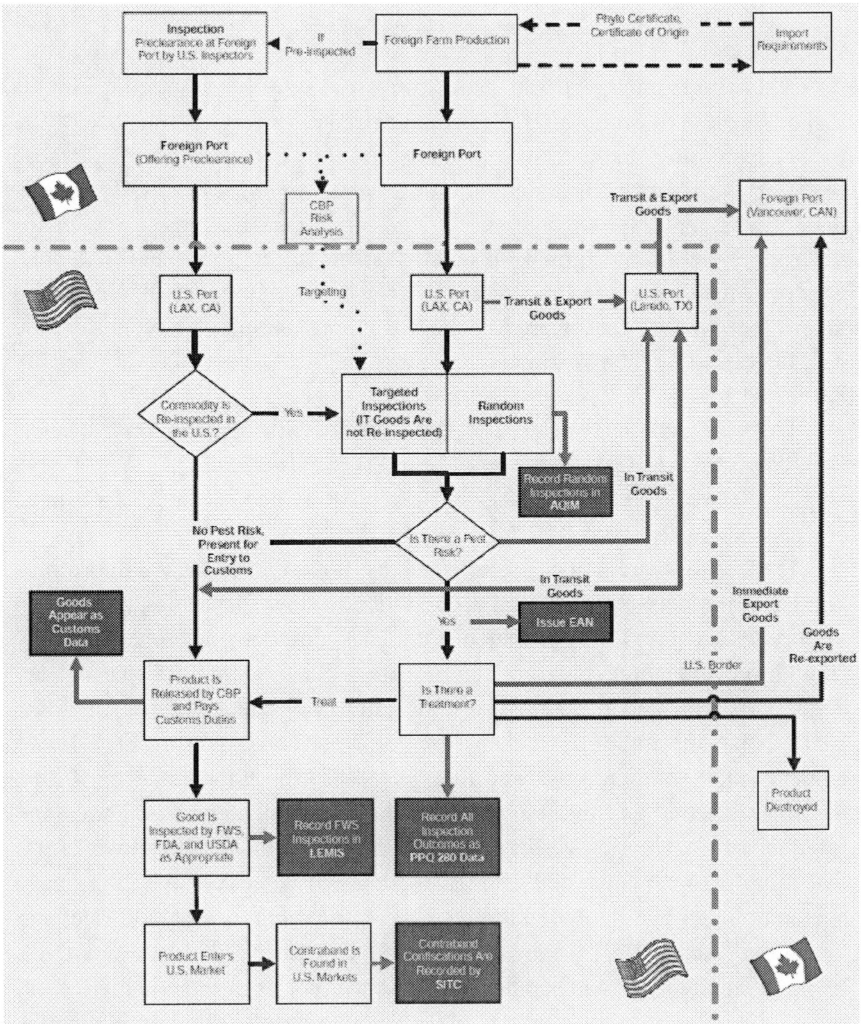

Source: USDA, Economic Research Service.

Figure 2. Import Inspections Data Collection.

Having cleared CBP, the first line of U.S. inspections, the goods may undergo further inspection by FWS (in the case of wildlife goods), the U.S. Food and Drug Administration, or other regulatory agencies.

Alternative Methods for Estimating the Size of Smuggling

Alternative methods for estimating the size of smuggling or its responsiveness to economic factors include those leveraging traceback data, those examining trade flow (or consumption) disparities, and those isolating the effect of anti-smuggling measures on stock prices. Traceback data are essentially an extremely rigorous inspection tool that helps determine the true origin or protected status of a good. For example, elephant tusks can be traced back to where they were harvested to determine whether they were poached. Random samples of ivory for sale can be traced to help estimate the percentage of ivory that is illegally harvested.

This method has primarily been used with endangered species, including whales (Dalebout et al., 2002), seals (Malik et al., 1997), elephants (Wasser et al., 2004), and agricultural goods, such as peanuts, coffee, and garlic (Ryan, 1998).

Trade flows are often documented by both the country importing a good and the country exporting a good. Trade flow disparities arise when imports and exports do not match. Ordinarily, random discrepancies may result from innocuous data collection errors, but systematic disparity may suggest that one country may be concealing the actual volume of trade. Using data on trade flow disparities, Fisman and Wei (2004) found evidence that smuggling is used to evade tariffs on goods entering China from Hong Kong and that smuggling is larger for higher value goods and for goods in categories with similar-looking substitutes with lower tariffs that might be mismanifested. Similar methods of detecting smuggling have been employed by Golub and Mbaye (2007) for sugar, wheat, and rice; and by Thursby et al. (1991), Saba et al. (1995), and Goel (2004) for cigarettes. In each application, substantial amounts of goods are smuggled from specific geographic areas and traded between a relatively limited number of partners.

Law-abiding companies will see their stock prices fall when embargoes are placed on their goods or when anti-smuggling measures are strengthened.

Alternatively, under these conditions, companies that smuggle will see their stock prices rise as the restrictions widen or extend the time period of the price wedge. DellaVigna and LaFerrara (2007) show mixed findings on the sensitivity of stock prices of weapons-producing companies that differ in their likeliness to smuggle in the face of U.N. embargoes on weapons sales to areas of civil conflict.

In addition to undergoing targeted inspections, goods are inspected randomly under the Agricultural Quarantine Inspection Monitoring Program (AQIM). Inspections data, covering both random and targeted inspections, represent the most comprehensive source of information on illegally imported goods. Other sources of data include the Pest ID data system, which records how pests found in shipments were identified, and the EAN database, which documents the alerts issued for the detection of prohibited goods or goods with pests. In all, four separate databases—PPQ 280 (USDA's record of agricultural cargo inspections outcomes), AQIM, Pest ID, and EAN—along with the Work Activities Data System (WADS) make up the Agricultural Quarantine Activities System (AQAS). This system is the primary tool for analysis of the risk posed by agricultural imports. USDA and CBP collect and share the data in real time.

Analysis of Agricultural and Wildlife Smuggling

Most analyses of illegal trade suffer from incomplete data, and, therefore, estimates of the size of illegal agricultural trade are subject to a great deal of error. For example, a TRAFFIC[11] source in Roe et al. (2002, pp. 10-12) writes:

> Any effort to describe the international wildlife trade must unfortunately begin with the recognition that this cannot be done with any accuracy.
>
> and
>
> The true size of the illegal (wildlife) trade is anyone's guess.

Similarly, FWS (2005, p. 2) writes that:

> ... though enforcement personnel know a great deal about what illegal trade activities occur locally, there is less understanding of illegal trade

activity nationally, or what might be occurring at other ports that could influence how interdiction efforts could be improved locally.

USDA has no official estimate of the total scope of agricultural smuggling. Severe methodological challenges complicate the estimation of illegal agricultural and wildlife trade with current data sources and limit the extent to which it can be characterized in an unbiased manner.

Analysis of USDA Random Inspections Data

USDA uses the AQIM program to improve the targeting of agricultural inspections and to assess the effectiveness of specific port operations. Under program protocol, ports are designated to randomly inspect certain goods received in large numbers and record the cargo's content, port of entry, origins, shipment contents, inspection method, pests found, and any indications of smuggling. AQIM inspections vary in levels of intensity. For example, an inspector might observe only the tailgate of a shipping container or truck, a proportion of the boxes drawn in a random sample, the entire contents of a part of the container, or the entire container's contents. These alternative methods of inspection may not reveal smuggling when it occurs. AQIM data have other limitations. First, many AQIM inspections involve goods that are not specifically agricultural, including floor tiles, machine parts, and wood packing material. Trade restrictions on these goods make them unlikely candidates for smuggling or for providing cover for other illicitly traded agricultural goods.[12] Second, AQIM inspections may not reveal smuggling even when performed correctly at the most rigorous level, especially in the case of goods having moved in trans-shipment. Also, actual inspection may be targeted toward the generally regular inspection goal of uncovering pests rather than smuggled goods. Third, AQIM inspections do not cover all agricultural goods, including, for example, meats. Fourth, a recent Government report indicates that some AQIM inspections in this time period may not have been conducted and recorded correctly (see OIG, 2007).

Based on AQIM data (obtained through an interagency agreement with APHIS), inspections rarely revealed smuggling between March 2003 and January 2007. Smuggling was detected only once in 4,605 inspections of southern U.S. border cargo, twice in 4,894 inspections of manufactured goods, and zero times in the 2,473 inspections of air cargo and 2,858 inspections of northern U.S. border cargo. Given the infrequent detection of smuggling, little inference can be made surrounding the scope of agricultural smuggling from these data, although random sampling methods have been used successfully elsewhere.[13]

Analysis of USDA Interdiction Data

Interdiction refers to the detection of illicitly traded goods in markets after they have entered the United States. While large resources are expended on the interdiction of narcotics and guns, far less is devoted exclusively to interdiction of illegally traded agricultural and wildlife goods. The APHIS Smuggling Interdiction and Trade Compliance (SITC) group comprises approximately 110 employees nationally who serve to recover goods that represent an SPS risk and have entered the U.S. supply chain. SITC prosecutes violators either through administrative or criminal punishments. In some cases, SITC focuses its efforts on recovering risky material, such as Spanish floor tile in wood packing material that was found to contain harmful wood-boring beetles in 2004. In these cases, no criminal intent is presumed.

Data on criminal interdiction are published in SITC's internal quarterly reports for the period 2002-06 and were obtained through interagency agreement with APHIS. These reports record each seizure by type, quantity, category, relevant Code of Federal Regulations violation for which the smuggler was penalized, and estimated value. Four types of goods are classified in the data: Animal and Meat Products,[14] Other Plant Products, Fruit Products, and Federal Noxious Weeds. Over the data-collection period, SITC expanded in size and budget and, subsequently, the number of interdictions also increased. Based on the data alone, it is difficult to determine whether interdicted goods are being sold in a commercial setting or used for personal consumption. For this reason, shipments valued at less than $50 were excluded from the following analysis.

Interdiction data are not random. Agents may target higher risk goods or exploit criminal networks, and they face administrative pressures to monitor certain goods more closely. As a result, data are likely to be biased toward easily observed, restricted goods that are obviously banned rather than goods that are regionally prohibited or easily misrepresented. Interdiction data are collected as part of ongoing interdiction efforts, and agents collect as much prohibited material as possible.

Tables 1-4 present interdiction data for the top five countries in each of these categories based on the number of interdictions between fiscal years

2002 and 2006. For the Fruit Products category and the Other Plant Products category, the three most commonly interdicted products for each country are identified. For Animal and Meat Products and Federal Noxious Weed categories, there is little difference across countries with regard to the types of identified goods.

In the Animal and Meat Products category, the data distinguish between pork, beef, poultry, or egg products with different levels of detail. Interdicted meat imports were particularly large from China, Japan, Korea, and India (table 1).

Alternatively, the low monetary value of interdictions from Mexico suggests that shipments might have been oriented toward individual personal consumption (rather than distribution), which APHIS staff indicate is common prior to holidays when immigrants bring specialty meats across the southern U.S. border. For the Fruit Products category, interdictions were also high with imports from Mexico, China, and Thailand (table 2).

For the Other Plant Products category, China has a disproportionately high number of interdictions, primarily involving shipments of szechuan pepper and citrus-based spice (table 3). Both of these goods may carry a variety of diseases that threaten citrus fruit, which has been an area of specialized focus following an outbreak of citrus canker in Florida in the late 1990s.

Table 1. Animal and meat product interdictions by SITC, 5-year totals (FY 2002-06)

Rank	Country of origin	Frequency	Value	Weight
		Number	Dollars	Pounds
1	China	175	866,151	262,920
2	Japan	60	355,056	36,888
3	Korea	44	150,111	22,843
4	Mexico	44	17,473	4,867
5	India	42	165,031	70,286
	Total	861	3,374,009	1,073,207

Source: USDA, Economic Research Service using USDA, Animal and Plant Health Inspection Service, Smuggling Interdiction and Trade Compliance (SITC) Quarterly Report (2002-06).

SITC interdiction data reveal a high likelihood for interdicted goods to be nontraditional, ethnic goods (specifically, spices) and to have a high value relative to their size.

Table 2. Fruit product interdictions by SITC, 5-year totals (FY 2002-06)

Rank	Country of origin	Frequency	Value	Weight	Top three items
		Number	Dollars	Pounds	
1	Mexico	60	94,426	69,840	Tejocotes, avocados, hog plums
2	China	32	75,044	39,437	Bael fruit, garlic,[1] ya pears
3	Thailand	26	8,047	2,776	Bael fruit, wood apple, krasang
4	Bangladesh	9	7,677	2,110	Satakora, citrus
5	Asia (unkown)	7	18,468	9,522	Citrus, longans, wood apple
	Total	190	556,447	209,049	Bael fruit, tejocotes, avocados

Source: USDA, Economic Research Service using USDA, Animal and Plant Health Inspection Service, Smuggling Interdiction and Trade Compliance (SITC) Quarterly Report (2002-06).

[1]In response to concerns that China was dumping low-priced garlic, the United States imposed a 377-percent tariff on Chinese garlic. Subsequently, interdictions periodically uncover trans-shipments of Chinese garlic (Kane, 2004).

Table 3. Other plant product interdictions by SITC, 5-year totals (FY 2002-06)

Rank	Country of origin	Frequency	Value	Weight	Top three items
		Number	Dollars	Pounds	
1	China	338	1,169,561	801,332	Szechuan pepper, citrus-based spice, burdock
2	India	140	116,842	51,895	Corn/millet, citrus-based spice, curcurbit
3	Mexico	125	192,462	33,098	Citrus-based spice, lemon grass, ruda
4	Thailand	64	69,263	71,932	Citrus-based spice, citrus, szechuan pepper
5	Korea	33	154,017	74,585	Corn/millet, lentil and citrus-based spice
	Total	897	2,193,803	1,170,664	Szechuan pepper, corn/millet, citrus

Source: USDA, Economic Research Service using USDA, Animal and Plant Health Inspection Service, Smuggling Interdiction and Trade Compliance (SITC) Quarterly Report (2002-06).

Table 4. Federal noxious weed interdictions by SITC, 5-year totals (FY 2002-06)

Rank	Country of origin	Frequency	Value	Weight
		Number	Dollars	Pounds
1	China	56	319,281	26,470
2	U.S. (domestic)	52	100,453	18,542
3	Thailand	29	46,505	9,743
4	Mexico	8	6,175	656
5	Vietnam	7	1,127	179
	Total	180	482,114	58,994

Source: USDA, Economic Research Service using APHIS-SITC Quarterly Report (2002-06).

This was evident in the Animal and Meat Products, Fruit Products, and Other Plant Products categories. Avocados represent an exception to this tendency, which is likely due to heightened political attention to avocado imports as trade of this product was liberalized over the period in question (APHIS, 2006).

Only a limited number of goods are considered Federal Noxious Weeds, a designation that indicates that the good's establishment and propagation make it an environmental threat by itself. For the countries in table 4, the top three goods for each were *solanum torvum* (turkey berry), *imperata cylindrical* (cogongrass, an ornamental grass), and *ipomea aquatica* (water spinach). Domestic transport accounts for a large share of Federal Noxious Weed interdictions, suggesting that internal trade is present. Given the infrequency of interdictions from Mexico and Vietnam, these observations are likely to be anomalous.

In terms of absolute monetary value, China is the largest source of interdicted material for trade, a finding that bears out over several product categories (table 5).

In terms of the value of interdicted goods to its legal trade, China also has the largest percentage15 of interdicted trade to legal trade (0.03 percent of total value), although the amount is not inordinately large relative to that for Japan, South Korea, and Taiwan. Although the percentages from each of the top 10 origin countries are small, it is important to recognize that this figure represents only a minimum level because the interdiction process almost certainly fails to uncover all smuggled goods. Moreover, certain factors may help explain why these countries have higher detected levels of smuggling.

Table 5. Total interdicted material and total agricultural imports, 5-year totals (FY 2002-06)

Rank	Country of origin	Interdicted material from 2002 to 2006	Agricultural imports from 2002 to 2006	Interdicted to total value ratio
			Thousand	
		Dollars	*dollars*	*Percent*
1	China	2,342,640	8,038,360	0.0291
2	Japan	374,562	2,063,320	0.0182
3	India	281,724	4,182,607	0.0068
4	South Korea	232,800	964,699	0.0241
5	Mexico	207,241	36,802,361	0.0006
6	Taiwan	184,844	904,963	0.0204
7	Thailand	136,705	5,171,291	0.0026
8	U.S. (domestic)	123,828	Not applicable	Not applicable
9	Canada	58,817	57,791,976	0.0001
10	Vietnam	56,261	1,731,613	0.0033

Source: USDA, Economic Research Service using USDA, Animal and Plant Health Inspection Service, Smuggling Interdiction and Trade Compliance (SITC) Quarterly Report (2002-06).

Asian countries, particularly China, have recently been recognized by the Federal Government as a source of potential invasive species because they have climates and habitats similar to those of the United States, they are home to a large variety of species that (unlike European species) have not been cultivated in the United States, and their volume of trade with the United States has increased significantly (Mack et al., 2002, p. 37). Based on the types of goods interdicted, it appears that illegally traded foods are most commonly discovered in ethnic food markets. The expansion of U.S. immigration in the 1990s, as well as the rise in food imports from China over the last 20 years, may have encouraged the growth of Asian ethnic food markets that support this trade.

The degree to which inspection and interdiction evidence is gathered is likely to depend on the ease with which smuggled goods are discovered. Inspectors and SITC officers may be more likely to identify contraband material if it is subject to a comprehensive ban based on the material's country of origin rather than just based on a region within a country. Frequently interdicted goods, such as szechuan pepper from China, fall under this criterion. Also, China has hosted two particularly large threats to U.S. agriculture—avian influenza and citrus diseases—that may have caused inspectors to pay closer attention to imports from China than from other countries.

Analysis of USDA Targeted Inspections Data

The outcomes of targeted agricultural inspections are collected in APHIS's PPQ 280 database, which is publicly available under the Freedom of Information Act. PPQ 280 data reveal the types of good, origin, quantity, and disposition code for plant agricultural goods physically inspected in the course of their importation to the United States. The disposition code indicates whether the shipment was inspected and whether pests were detected, but it does not indicate whether cargo concealed smuggled goods. Even if such distinctions were available, however, estimated percentages of goods that are smuggled would be biased upward because targeted inspections are oriented toward finding the maximum amount of prohibited material. Targeting factors and intensity of inspection efforts are not available in the data.

Using data from 1996 and 2006, this study isolates five disposition codes[16] that suggest that smuggling is being attempted,[17] including three codes for products that are prohibited and destroyed, returned, or assigned another action; one code for products destroyed due to a discrepancy with the shipment's phytosanitary certificate; and one code for products that are endangered species and sent to a rescue center.[18]

The sum of these shipments is herein called refused shipments. To avoid aggregation problems,[19] the focus of this analysis is on refused shipments of fruits and vegetables only. Table 6 provides findings for the top five countries ranked in terms of cumulative refused shipments of fruits and vegetables.

While Mexico has the largest amount of refused fruits and vegetables, it is also the largest source of fruit and vegetable imports to the United States. Mexico and China lead other nations in the number of shipments refused. While the rate of refusal for China is noticeably larger than that for Mexico, it is actually smaller than that for Argentina and Brazil.

Inspection data do not allow for a specific estimation of the size of smuggling but do indicate the types of goods that are refused because of suspected smuggling. These include citrus goods, tropical fruits (including papaya and mango), and ethnic foods (including szechuan pepper and ya pears). These varieties also overlap with the types of goods interdicted in markets as discussed in the previous section.

Table 6. Total refusals of shipments of fruits, vegetables, and spices (FY 1996-2006)

Country of origin	Shipments refused	Quantity refused, 1996-2006	Quantity imported, 2006	Top three goods refused, by number of shipments
	Number	Kilograms	Kilograms	
Mexico	1,418	8,346,009	3,952,110,724	Papaya (104), pepper (98), mango (97)
China	433	2,345,872	275,379,712	Citrus (130), szechuan pepper (104), ya pear (80)
Argentina	84	896,885	78,688,222	Citrus (24), mango (10), pear (5)
Brazil	74	1,129,368	103,591,410	Mango (42), papaya (12), citrus (9)
Spain	70	563,572	82,275,346	Pepper (31), citrus (21), cucumber (10)

Source: USDA, Economic Research Service using USDA, Animal and Plant Health Inspection Service PPQ 280 data (1996-2006) and U.S. Census Bureau data (2006).

Analysis of U.S. Fish and Wildlife Service Targeted Inspections Data

FWS (2005) used goods refused at import to characterize illegally traded wildlife goods based on entries in FWS's Law Enforcement Management Information System (LEMIS) declaration subsystem during 2000-04. The study explicitly acknowledged the known biases previously mentioned with APHIS inspections data. Refusals consist of goods that were given the disposition codes of seized, abandoned, or re-exported. While abandoned and re-exported goods suggest that trade might have been inadvertent, inspectors indicate that these goods are actually being traded illegally. The data collected through LEMIS are divided into the following taxonomic groups: reptiles, mammals, birds, mollusks, fish, coral, insects, amphibians, echinoderms, arachnids, crustaceans, and invertebrates. LEMIS data contain records on the number of goods imported each year as distinguished by country of origin, intended purpose (personal, commercial, hunting), estimated value (when possible), species, and size of shipment. Unlike goods under the PPQ 280 system, where the pest risk may be unknown when the good is imported, goods refused under the LEMIS system are known to be prohibited from entry into the United States.

Total refusals of wildlife goods in LEMIS data are disaggregated by purpose as follows: 61 percent for personal, 33 percent for commercial, 5 percent for hunting, and less than 2 percent for other reasons. Though the share of personal shipments refused each year (24 percent) is considerably higher than that of commercial shipments (1 percent) (FWS, 2005, p. 133), FWS does not distinguish between commercial and personal shipments in its detailed data reporting. The average refusal rate for all wildlife shipments was consistent at around 2.5 percent per year between 2000 and 2004, which includes both personal and cargo shipments. Note that about 24 percent of all wildlife shipments are inspected.[20] From the LEMIS data, it is difficult to determine the SPS risks posed by illegally traded wildlife. Certain types of frequently traded wildlife goods, such as animal leather, bones, and shells, are likely to pose a relatively small threat. Conversely, nonthreatened wildlife entering the United States legally may pose an SPS risk without causing a resource risk because quarantine and disease inspection measures are inadequate (for example, deer transported by U.S. hunters returning from Canada[21]).

Based on refusals in LEMIS data, the wildlife goods entering the United States with the highest percentage of refused entry are reptiles, coral, birds, and echinoderms (including starfish and sea cucumbers) (table 7). High refusal percentages for these goods are associated with a small volume of imports. This suggests that importers refrain from trading goods with a high probability of detection.

Based on primary use of refused goods, the following is evident. First, refused goods tend to be goods that are high in value relative to their size and might be characterized as luxuries, such as boots and shoes produced with alligator or crocodile leather, jewelry, and traditional medicines. Caviar was recently added to the CITES list of restricted species after Caspian Sea stocks grew extremely depleted, and illegal trade in caviar has been particularly problematic. Second, for most animal categories (except birds), the meat and live animal trade represents a relatively small portion of illegal trade, which is significant if these items have a greater SPS risk than other wildlife products, such as jewelry, leather, bone, and skin products.

Table 8 shows total refused wildlife imports as a proportion of total legal wildlife imports by country. The data do not distinguish between cargo and passenger shipments. Excluding the totals for Laos and Azerbaijan (whose wildlife trade is extremely small), Mexico is shown to have the highest rate of refusal of wildlife goods (and total number of refusals), but this finding is likely the result of the large amount of passenger travel between the United States and Mexico.[22]

After China, the percentage refused falls to 4.8 percent for Vietnam, the 11th-ranked country, whereas the median refusal rate for all countries is 4.0 percent. In terms of total refusals, Mexico, China, and Russia rank first, third, and sixth, respectively. For Mexico and Nicaragua, refused goods typically include live birds and snakes and leather products made from reptile skin. In these cases, the movement of live animals is of special concern, especially among birds, due to the potential of these animals to introduce diseases and pathogens into the United States.

Table 7. Number of wildlife shipments refused in FWS LEMIS data, 5-year totals (2000-04)

Category	Total cleared	Seized	Abandoned	Re-exported	Total refused	Total	Share refused	Primary uses of refused products
	Number						Percent	
Reptiles	85,379	3,255	1,267	641	5,163	90,542	5.7	Leather products, shoes
Coral	19,021	611	407	105	1,123	20,144	5.6	Raw and live coral
Birds	48,141	1,213	467	402	2,082	50,223	4.1	Live birds, feathers, trophies
Echino-derms	2,249	27	39	8	74	2,323	3.2	Bodies,* shells*
Mammals	218,353	3,146	1,322	528	4,996	223,349	2.2	Medicinals, skins, ivory
Fish	146,398	1,014	513	129	1,656	148,054	1.1	Caviar, live fish,* meat*
Mollusks	155,317	858	438	454	1,750	157,067	1.1	Shells for jewelry
All others	132,786	267	150	87	504	133,290	0.4	

Source: USDA, Economic Research Service using U.S. Fish and Wildlife Service (FWS), "U.S. Illegal Wildlife Trade" (2005, p. 6, table 7).

*Most of these products were regulated under domestic and foreign laws other than the Convention for the Trade of Endangered Species or the Endangered Species Act.

Table 8. Total refused shipments of wildlife by country of origin, 5-year totals (2000-04)

Rank	Country of origin	Cleared	Abandoned	Re-exported	Seized	Total	Total refused	Share refused
	------Number ---------							Percent
1	Laos	41	11	25	202	279	238	85.3
2	Azerbaijan	41	55	1	63	160	119	74.4
3	Mexico	9,641	1,743	229	1,800	13,413	3,772	28.1
4	Russia	2,149	252	13	297	2,711	562	20.7
5	Nigeria	1,415	151	7	165	1,738	323	18.6

Table 8. (Continued)

Rank	Country of origin	Cleared	Abandoned	Re-exported	Seized	Total	Total refused	Share refused
	------Number ---------							Percent
6	Nicaragua	776	17	23	111	927	151	16.3
7	El Salvador	1,240	46	3	131	1,420	180	12.7
8	Unknown	904	61	49	14	1,028	124	12.1
9	Marshall Islands	844	2	2	98	946	102	10.8
10	China	15,555	264	178	696	16,693	1,138	6.8

Source: USDA, Economic Research Service using U.S. Fish and Wildlife Service, "U.S. Illegal Wildlife Trade" (2005, p. 129, table 35).

Table 9. Value of legal and illegal trade in wildlife

		Illegal trade			Legal trade		Total trade	
Year	Lines refused	Value refused	Share with no value	Lines cleared	Value cleared	Share with no value	All shipments value	Share of total refused
	Number	*Dollars*	*Percent*	*Number*	*Dollars*	*Percent*	*Dollars*	*Percent*
2000	4,510	5,371,562[1]	26.4	259,629	1,702,763,815	11.0	1,713,435,377	0.6
2001	4,352	6,607,599[2]	22.2	310,508	1,468,274,339	10.1	1,475,381,938	0.5
2002	4,467	4,467,893	21.8	340,300	1,356,102,306	8.8	1,360,570,199	0.3
2003	4,712	4,381,595	28.5	375,200	1,512,419,944	9.2	1,516,801,539	0.3
2004	4,824	4,056,743	27.1	378,524	1,766,764,399[3]	6.6	2,770,821,142	0.2
Total		30,685,392			8,806,324,803		8,837,010,196	0.4

Source: USDA, Economic Research Service using U.S. Fish and Wildlife Service, "U.S. Illegal Wildlife Trade" (2005, p. 121, table 31).

[1]Excludes an outlier for ivory in 2000 valued at $5.3 million.

[2]Excludes an outlier for caviar in 2001 valued at $0.5 million.

[3]Excludes an outlier for a panda bear in 2004 value at $1 billion.

For China, refused goods often include traditional medicinal products made from a variety of animals as noted in Henry (2004) and Von Hippel and Von Hippel (2002). Refused goods from Russia often include caviar.

The proportion of the monetary value of the illegal wildlife trade to that of all wildlife trade is approximately 0.4 percent based on refusal data after correcting for data anomalies (table 9).[23] As with APHIS inspections data, if targeting occurs across the type of good imported, its origin, and its arrival conveyance, this estimate will be biased upward. However, no further adjustment is made to correct for this potential bias for several reasons. Unlike agricultural inspections, wildlife goods inspections are more specifically directed at uncovering illicit trade, making the reported rates of interception much more reliable. Little correlation exists in refusal and inspection rates across transport methods, which indicate that alternative transports likely receive the same level of scrutiny. Based on the number of shipments, a larger percentage (around 1 percent) of inspected commercial import entries than personal entries is refused (FWS, 2005, p. 133). Finally, there is no obvious manner in which this bias might be corrected.

The Characteristics of Agricultural and Wildlife Goods

This analysis supports three general conclusions. First, illegally traded agricultural goods are not those conventionally sold in supermarkets but tend to be specialty items with a high value relative to their size. Food items interdicted by APHIS are more likely to be ethnic foods and spices, such as szechuan pepper (a citrus-based spice), tejocotes (a Mexican crab apple), and ya pear (an Asian pear variety). Inspections data corroborate this finding somewhat, with szechuan pepper and ya pear being frequently found, along with citrus and high-value tropical fruits, including mango and papaya. Second, illegally traded wildlife goods are likely to be luxury items to be used for jewelry, reptile-leather shoes, and other products; caviar; and medicinal goods. Third, Mexico and China represent a large percentage of the detected illegal trade for wildlife and agricultural goods, respectively, though biological and geographical factors may help account for the different percentages across countries.

Conclusion

The recent passage of the Plant Protection Act and the Animal Health Protection Act reflects the ongoing concern in the United States over sanitary and phytosanitary concerns and resource risk in an era of increasing agricultural and wildlife imports and recent costly episodes of invasive species introductions. Inspections of imports play a crucial role in risk management, and U.S. inspection agencies have undergone significant consolidation since the creation of the U.S. Department of Homeland Security in 2003. Several findings emerge from the examination of import refusals and interdiction data from APHIS and FWS. Illegal agricultural imports are driven primarily by specialty markets for ethnic foods and may reflect the general idiosyncrasies of agricultural trade prohibitions and enforcement. Illegal wildlife imports are driven by the trade in luxury items and jewelry, including leather products; culturally specific traditional medicines; ivory; caviar; and shell jewelry. These types of imports are also likely to command high prices relative to their cost and size, which is not surprising given the profit motive of smuggling.

Smuggling of wildlife into the United States is most prevalent with Mexico, and smuggling of agricultural products is most prevalent with China. Both countries are major trade partners with the United States, and U.S. imports from both increased dramatically over the last 25 years. Similarly, immigration may have increased the prevalence of ethnic food, traditional goods, and medicinal goods that seem to be especially associated with illegal trade. In terms of size, detected illegal trade seems to be a significant part of the total wildlife trade and a smaller but nontrivial part of the agricultural trade. Based on the fragmentary inspection evidence, the illegal wildlife trade is approximately 1 percent of commercial wildlife shipments and 0.4 percent of the total value of the wildlife trade. Based on fragmentary interdiction evidence, the illegal agricultural trade has a lower bound of approximately 0.03 percent of total agricultural trade for China, which had the highest reported proportions and volumes. Still, these figures, along with most widely reported public estimates, are inexact due to the potential for bias in the data.

Concerns over smuggling extend beyond risks surrounding invasive species or endangered wildlife. Expertise across different fields, including international law, criminology, economics, agricultural sciences, pathology, and environmental science, is necessary to formulate an impartial and comprehensive regulatory and enforcement regime. Idiosyncratic factors influence the need for individual regulations, yet the nature of inspections and border security has necessitated that risks from imports—SPS, resource, or other national security interests—be addressed in a unified manner. A better understanding of the incentives to smuggle goods is emerging and will aid further research efforts as markets and supply chains become more integrated.

ACKNOWLEDGMENTS

The author thanks Ron Komsa, Scott Sanner, Willy Harris, and Nolan Lemon of USDA's Animal and Plant Health Inspection Service and Craig Hoover of the U.S. Department of the Interior's Fish and Wildlife Service for assistance in understanding the statistics and regulatory structure described in this report. Thanks also for the helpful comments of Donna Roberts, Craig Osteen, and Barry Krissoff of USDA's Economic Research Service; Lori Lynch of the University of Maryland's Department of Agricultural and Resource Economics; and Holly Ameden of the University of California at Berkeley. Any errors are those of the author.

References

Becker, Gary S. "Crime and Punishment: An Economic Approach," *Journal of Political Economy,* 76(1968)2:169-217.

Bhagwati, J., and B. Hensen. "A Theoretical Analysis of Smuggling," *Quarterly Journal of Economics,* 87(1973)2:172-187.

Bushway, S., and P. Reuter. "Economists' Contribution to the Study of Crime and the Criminal Justice System," in Michael Torny (ed.), *Crime and Justice, Volume 37: A Review of Research,* University of Chicago Press, 2008.

Caulkins, J.P., and P. Reuter. "Illicit Drug Markets and Economic Irregularities," *Socio-Economic Planning Sciences,* 40(2006):1-14.

Caulkins, J.P., and P. Reuter. "What Price Data Tells Us About Drug Markets," *Journal of Drug Issues,* 28(1998)3:593-612.

Convention on International Trade in Endangered Species of Wild Fauna and Flora. *Appendix I, II, and III,* http://www.cites.org/eng/app/E-Jul01. pdf, current as of July 2008.

Dalebout, M.L., G.M. Lento, F. Cipriano, N. Fubahashi, and C.S. Baker. "How Many Protected Minke Whales Are Sold in Japan and Korea? A Census by Microsatellite DNA Profiling?" *Animal Conservation,* 5(2002)143-152

DellaVigna, S., and E. La Ferrara. "Detecting Illegal Arms Trade," NBER Working Paper 13355, August 2007.*The Economist.* "Easy Money," September 21, 2006.

Feinstein, J. "Approaches for Estimating Noncompliance: Examples from Federal Taxation in the United States," *The Economic Journal,* 109(1999)456:360-369.

Ferrier, P. "Illicit Agricultural Trade," *Agricultural and Resource Economic Review,* 37(2008):2.

Fischer, C. "The Complex Interactions of Markets for Endangered Species Products," *Journal of Environmental Economics and Management,* 48(2004):926-953.

Fischer, C. "Trading in Endangered Species: Legal Sales Versus Total Bans," *Resources,* 150(2003):12-14.

Fisman, R., and S. Wei. "Tax Rates and Tax Evasion: Evidence from 'Missing Imports' in China," *Journal of Political Economy,* 112(2004)2:471-496.

Fisman, R., and S. Wei. "The Smuggling of Art, and The Art of Smuggling: Uncovering the Illicit Trade in Cultural Properties and Antiques," NBER Working Paper 13446, 2007.

Goel, R.K. "Cigarette Demand in Canada and the U.S.: Canadian Cigarette Smuggling," *Applied Economic Letters,* 11(2004):537-540.

Golub, S., and A. Mbaye. "Colonial History, Regional Integration and Smuggling in South Africa: The Case of The Gambia," Swarthmore College Working Paper, June 2007.

Hansen, Eric. *Orchid Fever,* Random House Books, 2000.

Heltberg, R. "Impact of the Ivory Trade Ban on Poaching Incentives: A Numerical Example," *Ecological Economics,* 36(2001):189-195.

Henry, L. "A Tale of Two Cities: A Comparative Study of Traditional Chinese Medicine Markets in San Francisco and New York City," TRAFFIC North America: World Wildlife Fund, 2004.

Howse, R. "The Appellate Body Ruling in the Shrimp/Turtle Case: A New Legal Baseline in Trade and Environmental Debate," 27 *Columbia Review of Law* (2002) 489.

Hutton, J. "Who Knows Best? Controversy of Unilateral Stricter Domestic Measures," in *Endangered Species, Threatened Convention: The Past, Present and Future,* J. Hutton and B. Dickson (eds.), Earthscan Ltd., 2000.

Interpol. Personal communication, October 2006.

Interpol. *Wildlife Crime*, http://www.interpol.int, accessed April 10, 2008.

Ivanova, K. "Corruption, Illegal Trade, and Compliance with the Montreal Protocol," *Environmental Resource Economics,* (2007) 38:475-496.

Jacob, B., and S. Levitt. "Rotten Apples: An Investigation of the Prevalence and Predictors of Teacher Cheating," *Quarterly Journal of Economics,* 118(2003)3: 843-877.

Kane, L. "A Recipe for Scampi - How It Really Gets To Your Table," *Customs and Border Patrol Today*, December 2004, http://www.cbp. gov/ xp/CustomsToday/2004/Dec/commoditytrail.xml.

Karesh, W.B., R.B. Cook, E.L. Bennet, and J. Newcomb. "Wildlife Trade and Global Disease Emergence," *Emerging Infectious Disease,* 11(2005)7:1000-1002.

Kemp, M. "Smuggling and Optimal Commercial Policy," *Journal of Public Economics,* 5(1976)3:381-384.

Kremer, M., and C. Morcom. "Elephants," *American Economic Review*, 90(2000)1:212-234.

Levitt, S.D. "Using Electoral Cycles in Police Hiring to Estimate the Effect of Police on Crime," *American Economic Review*, 87(1997)3:270-290.

Lynch, L., and E. Lichtenberg. "Foreword: Special Issue on Invasive Species," *Agricultural and Resource Economics Review*, 35(2006)1:iii-v.

Mack, R.N., S.C.H. Barrett, P.L. deFur, W.L. MacDonald, L.V. Madden, D.S. Marshall, D.G. McCullough, P.B. McEvoy, J.P. Nyrop, S.E.H. Reichard, K.J. Rice, and S.A. Tolin. *Predicting Invasions of Non-Indigenous Plants and Plant Pests*, National Research Council, National Academy Press, 2002.

Malik, S., P.J. Wilson, R.J. Smith, D.M. Lavigne, and B.N. White. "Pinniped Penises in Trade: A Molecular-Genetic Investigation," *Conservation Biology*, 11(1997)6:1365-1374.

Martin, L., and Panagariya, A. "Smuggling, Trade and Price Disparity," *Journal of International Economics,* 117(1984)3:4:201-217.

Martin, R.B. "When CITES Works and When It Does Not," in *Endangered Species, Threatened Convention: The Past, Present and Future*, John Hutton and Barnabas Dickson (eds.), Earthscan Ltd., 2000.

Meissner, H., A. Lemay, T. Kalaris, J. Vila, R. Duncan, and R. Olive. *Mexican Border Risk Analysis*, Plant Epidemiology and Risk Analysis Laboratory, Center for Plant Health Science and Technology, 2003.

Min, H., M. Gopinath, S. Buccola, and P. McEvoy. "Rent-Seeking in Invasive Species Regulation: The Case of Noxious Weeds," *Land Economics*, 84 (2): 306-326.

Naim, M. *Illicit: How Smugglers, Traffickers and Copycats Are Hijacking the Global Economy,* Doubleday, 2000.

Norton, D. "On the Economic Theory of Smuggling," *Economica,* 55(1988)217:107-118.

Reed, Robert, N. "An Ecological Risk Assessment of Nonnative Boas and Pythons as Potentially Invasive Species in the United States," *Risk Analysis,* 25(2005)3: 753-766.

Roe, D., Mulliken, T., and Milledge S. (eds.). *Making a Killing or Making a Living: Wildlife Trade, Trade Controls and Rural Livelihoods*, IIED and UCN, London, UK, 2002.

Ryan, M.A. "Finding Food Imposters: It's Not Just Peanuts," *Today's Chemist at Work,* 7(1998)6:63-66, http://pubs.acs.org/hotartcl/tcaw/98/ jun/fin. html.

Saba, R.P., R.T. Beard, and R.B. Ekelund. "The Demand For Cigarette Smuggling," *Economic Inquiry,* 33(1995):189-202.

Strumpf, K. *Illegal Sports Bookmakers*, University of North Carolina Working Paper, 2003.

Thursby, M., R. Jensen, and J. Thursby. "Smuggling, Camouflaging, and Market Structure," *Quarterly Journal of Economics,* 106(1991)3:789-814.

U.S. Department of Agriculture, Agricultural Marketing Service (AMS). *Agricultural Export Transportation Handbook,* Agriculture Handbook 700, 2004.

U.S. Department of Agriculture, Animal and Plant Health Inspection Service (APHIS). Personal communication, USDA-APHIS-SITC Staff in Raleigh, NC, August 2006.

U.S. Department of Agriculture, Animal and Plant Health Inspection Service (APHIS). "APHIS Preclearance Programs," Revised March 24, 2004, on file with author and available at: www.aphis.usda.gov/ import_export/ plants/plant_imports/downloads/preclearance_chart.pdf.

U.S. Department of Commerce, Census Bureau (Census Bureau). *U.S. Imports of Merchandise*, various years.

U.S. Department of Homeland Security, Customs and Border Protection (CBP). "Customs and Border Patrol Press Kit: Agriculture," www.cbp. gov/xp/cgov/newsroom/fact_sheets/cbp_overview/press_kit/, accessed May 10, 2007a.

U.S. Department of Homeland Security, Customs and Border Protection (CBP). Personal communication, Port of Baltimore Agricultural Inspectors, September 21, 2007b.

U.S. Department of Homeland Security, Customs and Border Protection (CBP). "U.S. Customs and Border Patrol Interception of Illegal Citrus Cuttings Becomes First Felony Conviction in Violations of the Plant Protection Act of 2005," Press release dated September 9, 2005.

U.S. Department of the Interior, Fish and Wildlife Service, Office of Law Enforcement Intelligence Unit (FWS). *U.S. Wildlife Trade: An Overview for 1997-2003*, 2003, www.fws.gov/le/pdffiles/Wildlife Trade Overview Report.pdf.

U.S. Department of the Interior, Fish and Wildlife Service (FWS). "U.S. Illegal Wildlife Trade: LEMIS Data Analysis and Risk Assessment," Internal FWS Report, November 2005.

U.S. Department of the Interior, Fish and Wildlife Service (FWS). Personal correspondence regarding import/shipments recorded in LEMIS, December 2008.

U.S. Government Accountability Office (GAO). *Homeland Security Office: Management and Coordination Problems Increase the Vulnerability of U.S. Agriculture to Foreign Pests and Disease*, GAO-Report 06-664, 2006, www.gao.gov/new.items/d06644.pdf

U.S. Government Accountability Office (GAO). *Persistent Weaknesses in the In-Bond Cargo System Impede Customs and Border Protection's Ability to Address Revenue, Trade, and Security Concerns*, GAO-Report 07-561, 2007, www.gao.gov/new.items/d07561.pdf

U.S. Departments of Agriculture and Homeland Security, Offices of the Inspector Generals (OIG). "Review of Customs and Border Protection's Agriculture Inspection Activities," Report OIG-07-32, February 2007, www.dhs.gov/xoig/assets/mgmtrpts/OIG_07-32_ Feb07.pdf.

U.S. Office of Technology Assessment (OTA). *Harmful Non-indigenous Species in the United States*, OTAF-F-565, 1993.

Von Hippel, F.A., and W. Von Hippel. "Sex Drugs and Animal Parts: Will Viagara Save Threatened Species?" *Environmental Conservation,* 29(2002)3:277-281.

Von Kooten, G.C. "A Dynamic Bioeconomic Model of Ivory Trade: Details and Extended Results," Working Paper #2006-03, University of Victoria, Department of Economics, Victoria, BC, Canada, 2006.

Wasser, S.K., A.M. Shedlock, K. Comstock, E.A. Ostrander, B. Mutayoba, M. Stephens. "Assigning African Elephant DNA to Geographic Region of Origin: Application to the Ivory Trade," *Proceedings of the National Academy of Sciences,* 101(2004)14847-14852, http://www.pnas.org/cgi/content/full/101/41/14847.

Yang, D. "Can Enforcement Backfire? Crime Displacement in the Context of Customs Reform in the Philippines," *The Review of Economics and Statistics,* 90(2008)1:1-14.

End Notes

[1] Exact sourcing of Interpol's reported estimates on this figure is unclear. Malik et al. (1997), for example, state that the total value of all trade in wildlife, not just illegal products, is $8 billion to $20 billion.

[2] Karesh et al. (2005) show that contact with animals in illegal markets substantially encourages transmission of wildlife-to-livestock, wildlife-tohuman, and wildlife-to-wildlife diseases,

such as severe acute respiratory syndrome (SARS), avian influenza, (avian) paramyxovirus, monkeypox (in rodents), and chytriodiomycosis (in wild amphibians). Reed (2005) notes that illegally wild-caught boa constrictors are more likely to carry zoonotic diseases, such as Salmonella on hitchhiking ticks, and that wild species are also likely to be more invasive if accidentally released in the wild, as has happened with boa constrictors in the Florida Everglades. Endangered live plants (such as orchids, cacti, and cycads) are periodically wild-harvested and transported in native soils, which might themselves contain a variety of invasive species.

[3] CITES and most sources on the illegal trade assume that smuggling is harmful prima facie. Hutton (2000), Martin (2000), Kremer and Morcom (2000), and Malik et al. (1997) argue that freer, sanctioned trade will create better incentives for developing countries to preserve sustainable harvests of wildlife in specific cases. This argument does not support illegal trade but argues for reduction in trade prohibitions.

[4] Health effects are likely to occur with meats, such as beef from countries with bovine spongiform encephalopathy (BSE) and poultry from countries with avian influenza. For plant products, most pests are not a threat to human health. Contamination and adulteration risk, primarily under the domain of the U.S. Food and Drug Administration, is still likely here, but these goods are more likely to be sold fraudulently rather than be smuggled (in an informed two-party transaction).

[5] Fischer (2004; 2003), Von Kooten (2006), and Heltberg (2001) all address stigma effects in their discussion of the illegal wildlife trade.

[6] Henry (2004) finds that approximately 50 percent of selected stores surveyed offered traditional Chinese medicines, products for medical use labeled as containing animal parts controlled under CITES or the Endangered Species Act.

[7] Members of the North American Free Trade Agreement (NAFTA) can appeal cases to NAFTA's independent dispute resolution mechanism before going to the World Trade Organization.

[8] The Lacey Act prohibiting "the import, export, transportation, sale, receipt, acquisition, or purchase of fish, wildlife, or plants taken, possessed, transported, or sold in violation of any Federal, State, tribal, or foreign law" is also typically invoked when illegal trade is actually uncovered.

[9] The General Agreement on Tariffs and Trade contains similar language allowing member countries to enact trade restrictions necessary for "conservation of exhaustible natural resources" while also requiring that they be nondiscriminatory. See Howse (2002) for a discussion of whether restrictions may be applied to production methods.

[10] Generally, regulated agricultural cargo must be inspected for pest risk to enter the United States, whereas unregulated cargo and cargo entering under the National Agricultural Release Program does not. Obviously, cargo that would be prohibited can be mismanifested as unregulated cargo.

[11] TRAFFIC is a joint program of the World Wildlife Fund and the World Conservation Union.

[12] Because machine parts and floor tile have carried hitchhiker pests in the past, they are randomly inspected for compliance with packaging protocols. The cargo containers carrying these goods are not refrigerated and are therefore unlikely to be suitable for the transportation of most agricultural goods.

[13] Specifically, Jacob and Levitt (2003) used the method for re-testing and Feinstein (1999) used the method for auditing.

[14] The Animal Products and Meat Products categories were combined from the original data because their goods overlapped significantly.

[15] Ivanova (2007) similarly fi nds that China is the largest source of illicit traded ozone-depleting substances prohibited under international agreement.

[16] These codes are DEPP, OTPP, and RXPP for the goods that were prohibited products; DEPD for the goods rejected for having phyto discrepancies; and ESRC for goods confiscated for being endangered species.

[17] Although APHIS staff indicate that attempting to import prohibited goods is suggestive of smuggling, import shipments may still receive these disposition codes when the goods are correctly manifested. Typically, APHIS does not consider goods as being smuggled unless there is intent to conceal the true contents.

[18] The relatively small number of endangered plant species include orchids, cacti, and cycads.

[19] Cut flower and propagative material imports are measured in stems and plant units rather than by weight and are difficult to interpret in terms of volume

[20] Isolating commercial shipments to arrive only from air cargo, ocean cargo, mail, rail, or truck changes this figure from 24 to 25 percent (FWS, 2005, pg. 137).

[21] USDA enacted several restrictions on Canadian wildlife imports after the 2003 discovery of bovine spongiform encephalopathy in a Canadian dairy cow.

[22] FWS (2005, p. 128) also notes that "the high number and rate of refusal (28.1 percent) for imports from Mexico is largely due to the strict prohibitions against export of most wildlife without permits, coupled with a vibrant trade in a variety of protected species products such as reptile skin boots."

[23] In table 9, "lines refused" refers to shipment entries refused. "Share with no value" refers to the percentage of imports that have no recorded import value because they cannot be legally sold (FWS, 2005, p. 122).

INDEX

C

F

G

H

L

M

N

O

P

R

S

Y

Z